From the Bluegrass to the Balkans

Living, Loving, and Leaving Macedonia

By Benjamin Shultz

Copyright © 2016 by Benjamin Shultz

All rights reserved. No part of this publication may be reproduced, distributed, or transmitted in any form or by any means, including photocopying, recording, or other electronic or mechanical methods, without the prior written permission of the publisher, except in the case of brief quotations embodied in critical reviews and certain other noncommercial uses permitted by copyright law.

Cover Photo Copyright © 2016 by Vlado Krstevski
All rights reserved.
More photos and contact information available at
www.vladokrstevski.com

За Оливер

Еден дел од моето срце ќе биде секогаш со тебе во Македонија

TABLE OF CONTENTS

Part I: On Culture

1. From the Bluegrass to the Balkans — 1
2. Europe's Obscure and Uncharted Frontier — 17
3. Makedonska Rabota: Getting by in Daily Life — 36
4. Celebrating Life, Celebrating Family — 62

Part II: On Institutions

5. The Paradox, and Promise, of Education in the Global Era — 80
6. Yugonostalgia and Capitalism in Europe's Wild, Wild East — 100
7. Politics is Everything, and Everything is Politics — 125
8. The New Macedonian Question — 146

Part III: On Leaving

9. The Next New Beginning — 166

Glossary – A Foreigner's Guide to Basic Macedonian — 176

PART I

On Culture

CHAPTER 1

From the Bluegrass to the Balkans

Back home in the United States, the standard response I get when I tell people that I was living in Macedonia is a slow and hesitant, "Ohhhh... yeah." I can see from their cautious reaction that the word "Macedonia" is familiar enough that they feel a moment of slight embarrassment when they realize that beyond having heard the name, they know exactly zero additional details. I learned to say that I was living in Eastern Europe, and if that elicited a follow-up question, I would say next to Greece, because let's face it, people have at least some mental image of Greece. On rare occasions, someone will say, "Oh sure, I was in Kosovo and we used to go to Macedonia all the time," or "I know all about Macedonia from my time in Bosnia." Any time I hear that, I immediately know that they are referring to their time in the military, not their epic road trip through the Balkans. Leaving Americans' generally low level of geographic knowledge aside, this is somewhat to be expected given Macedonia's small size, population, and global political footprint. I have two graduate degrees in geography and I also could not have said anything intelligent about the place before moving there for love in 2013.

At the time I was 31-years-old, and when I showed up in the country I had no solid job prospects there, no knowledge of the language, and no idea of what to expect. I didn't even have a residential permit. I had recently completed a PhD in geography and was doing adjunct teaching jobs while I applied for more stable tenure-track positions. When my girlfriend (now wife) needed to go back to Macedonia because of visa restrictions in the United States, I was faced with a choice. I could continue trying to climb the brutal academic ladder in America and chase relatively low-paying jobs to places where I did not particularly want to live. Or, I could take a huge risk and quit my adjunct job so I could move to one of Europe's poorest countries and continue our relationship while I tried to find work there. For me, the choice was clear.

After all, I had already established a track record of setting out into the unknown. The first time I ever got onto a plane I was 15-years old, and the destination was Bogota, Colombia. I had never really been all that far from my home state of Kentucky prior to that. The year was 1997, just a few years removed from the violence of Pablo Escobar and the cartel wars that took tens of thousands of lives. I was visiting a friend who had been an exchange student at my high school the year prior. He invited me and I somehow I convinced my parents to get me a passport and a plane ticket. In retrospect, it's easy to question the wisdom of their decision to let me go given the stability of Colombia at that time, but the experience gave me a wanderlust that I have never been able to shake.

Two years later I went to Costa Rica and stayed for almost a year. Since visiting Colombia I had developed a strong interest in Spanish, and when I met a man from Costa Rica who moved to my hometown in Kentucky, he recommended that I go there to improve my language ability. He arranged a sort of informal exchange with a host family there that consisted of me living at their house for a year and their son living at my house the following year. Given the informal nature of the arrangement, I still don't know how both sides managed to actually keep up their end of the agreement, but we did. We still keep in touch to this day. A few years later I went on a one-semester exchange to Italy, which once again put me in the position of being in a new place with a new language and having no contacts. I studied at the medieval University of Pavia and took four classes in Italian, a language that I had a rudimentary knowledge of when I arrived and a moderate proficiency of when I left.

The reason I am pointing these things out is to say that when I made the decision to move to Macedonia, I felt like I had a good handle on how things were going to be. I had traveled before and understood that the world beyond the borders of the United States was vast and distinct. I had successfully learned foreign languages by immersing myself and figuring things out on my own. I felt prepared, confident, and ready for a new challenge. Like in my previous experiences living abroad, I assumed I would struggle at first with the language and slowly improve, all the while picking up on the little idiosyncrasies of life in a new place and eventually settling right in. That is what was supposed to happen. After living there full-time for three years, I now realize how wrong my calculation was. Macedonia is, without a doubt, the most different place I have ever lived.

In fairness, I was warned. Through various soccer teams back in the United States I befriended people from the Balkans and other Eastern European countries. When we discussed my plan to move to Macedonia they universally, even adamantly, advised against it. They would tell me stories of having to work through personal connections just to get basic services and bureaucratic things done, and the necessity of having a political membership card to even be considered for employment in many places. They would tell me stories about paychecks being weeks or even months late, and in some cases longer. They told me it's harder to live there than I think it is, and that I'm better off staying away. Everyone from there wanted to come to the United States, and here I was an American citizen with my life in front of me and I wanted to go there?

To be honest, I thought that they were making these things up, or at least embellishing the details. How was it possible, I asked myself, to actually have physical political party cards as a precondition of employment in a 21st century European democracy? I assumed that was the way things worked during the communist time, but surely this was an exaggeration in today's world. How could a company just not pay its employees for months at a time, and why did the employees or the government not do something about that? Call it a personality quirk, but with every story I heard about how hard life is in the Balkans, my desire to go see for myself grew. I saw it as sort of challenge to go thrive in a place where everyone says it's too difficult to make it. I made up my mind, and in 2012 started putting together a plan to move to Macedonia the following year for an indefinite amount of time.

Shortly thereafter, Macedonia started pushing back. From the moment I started trying to line up my residential visa, I realized that maybe my Eastern European friends were not completely exaggerating. Six or seven months prior to my planned moving date, I looked up the number for the Macedonian embassy in Washington, DC and gave them a call. After a few rings, I heard, "Hello?"

Not expecting someone in an official capacity at an embassy to answer the phone with a simple "hello," I thought maybe I called the wrong number.

"Is this the Macedonian embassy?" I asked.

"Yes," said the voice abruptly on the other end.

"Ok... I'd like to ask about the process for applying for a residential visa," I said, still not one hundred percent confident that I had called the right place.

"What do you mean residential visa? We don't do that," he told me in a confused voice.

"If you don't deal with visas, then who does?"

"I don't know, try our consulate in Chicago, they can answer your questions," he told me, and hung up. Strike one, I thought. Maybe it was my mistake, maybe my ignorance of the visa application process led me to the wrong office.

Undeterred, a quick Internet search turned up the number for the Chicago consulate and I called. The phone rang... and rang... and rang. Even though I thought it was strange that a government agency would not have someone to answer the phone during normal business hours on a week day, I waited for about an hour and called back. When someone eventually answered and we went through a similar, though slightly more professional routine, I was directed to the New York consulate and told that they would answer my questions.

"Hello?"

"Is this the Macedonian consulate in New York?"

"Yes."

Once again I explained that I would like information on how to apply for a residential visa to live in Macedonia. He asked me when I am planning on moving, and I told him in about six or seven months. Sounding incredulous, he asked me why I was applying so early. I explained that I just wanted to be ready because getting a residential visa for a new country seems like a lengthy process. He assured me it was not, and that I was too early, but sent me the forms anyway, and that was that. They were scans of photocopies of photocopies, bearing the marks of a document that had been used over and over again. The whole application was a mere four pages, and they looked so unofficial that I was not completely sure if they were even real.

After I started looking at the forms, I realized there were no additional instructions. For example, what do I do with the application once I fill it out? What is the next step? I made the Washington-Chicago-New York phone circuit a few more times and we came to the conclusion that maybe it was better if I just applied after I got there. The person on the phone told me it was just too unusual to apply for a visa that far out, without even being in the country, and assured me that I would have no problem getting one upon arrival. Doubt started to creep in, but there was simply no way I was going to let the system beat me and prove everyone right before I ever set foot in the place. I was determined to push on, and so in January of 2013 I boarded a plane and flew to Macedonia with two suitcases full of everything I could pack. More than 14 hours later, I landed in what was to be my home for the next three years.

People often ask me what I thought about the country before going there, as in what did I imagine it to be like. Macedonia at that time fit into any of the undifferentiated, generic images I had of Eastern Europe. I knew it was poor, I knew it was in the old communist bloc, and I knew it was different from Western Europe. I also knew that every now and then on television and in the news it was referred as the Former Yugoslav Republic of Macedonia, but I did not know why and I really did not care to find out. Beyond that, Macedonia was essentially a blank slate for me, which was refreshing because it meant I could form my own opinions on the place without the burden of bias or prejudice. I was truly going out into the unknown, and it was pretty exciting.

 My crash course in all things Macedonia started on the car ride from the airport as we were going to meet my wife's family. Looking out the window I remember thinking ok, this is not so different from the other developing countries I've been to. Broken roads, untended lawns, small cars, and the occasional horse-drawn cart among the regular traffic are pretty standard for some parts of the world. I was taking it all in stride, and as we approached Skopje I started to get a sense of the city's quirky physical appearance. Feral cats and dogs roamed freely in the broken and dusty streets alongside a few Renault 4s, Zastavas, and Yugos from the 1960s and 1970s, which somehow still run after decades of use and repair. Rusting factory complexes were scattered throughout the urban expanse in a way that would not be out of place in the American Rust Belt. As I later learned, those factories contribute to a dense smog that can reduce visibility down to just a few feet in the winter months. Skopje is, in fact, one of the most polluted cities in Europe, and can on occasion look and smell as if it is downwind from a massive forest fire.

We turned off the main road and onto a narrow residential street, driving by old housing barracks and visibly dilapidated buildings from the socialist era. They provide a stark contrast next to gleaming shopping malls, brand new apartment buildings, and the most modern, clean gas stations I have ever seen. Seriously, the gas stations look like they were designed on the set of a movie about the perfect community that is hiding a ghastly secret. As we snaked our way through the neighborhood, I looked up at a towering 17-story apartment building that seemed in particularly poor condition and pursed my lips to say, "Surely people don't actually live in that building." Before the words ever left my mouth, one of the people riding with us in the car said, "That's my building! We're here!" I felt a sense of relief that I had kept my mouth shut for once.

Not one minute after my near brush with embarrassment, we parked the car outside of my future in-laws' building. On the walk to meet them for the first time, I came across the smallest, strangest-looking car I had ever seen. It looked like the sort of aging relic of communism that I had seen in photos, and I excitedly asked my girlfriend to take my picture next to it so I could show my friends back home. She laughed and said, "That's my dad's car!" as she snapped a picture of me towering over his green "*peglica*," otherwise known as a Fiat 126. To this day that remains one of my favorite photos from my time there. After that I took a photo of a Roma man sorting through the trash can next to his horse and cart, and then of another rundown apartment building where people still live.

    I often cringe when looking back at my first photos of Macedonia. It is obvious to me that I went in ready to confirm my preconceived notions of Eastern Europe that I had internalized from the film *Borat* and old Soviet stereotypes. The song playing in the opening credits of *Borat*, after all, is by a well-known Macedonian folk artist. As traveled and as cosmopolitan as I believed myself to be, I was unprepared and uninformed, not so different from the members of the American media that covered the 2014 Winter Olympics in Sochi, Russia. Just like I had done, they began searching for ways to perpetuate a narrative of Eastern European backwardness almost as soon as they arrived. The hashtag #sochiproblems became an online sensation even before the games began, shifting the focus away from sport and towards shoddy construction, stray cats and dogs, and a shortage of resources. While those aspects of the Olympics and Russia itself deserved to be exposed, they were mostly presented as inconvenient yet comical sideshows for foreign visitors who would be leaving all that mess behind soon enough.

    Seeing the media coverage from afar, one might be excused for overlooking the fact that political corruption and financial instability actually do characterize the daily lives of millions of people throughout Eastern Europe, and not just when the international press is in town. Those who are still struggling to find their feet in the transition from socialism to capitalism find creative ways to make do with what they have and attempt to live out their hopes and dreams, just like everyone else. Weary of the lack of progress, thousands of young people have left the region in search of better opportunities abroad, and many of them will never return.

Paradoxically, the idea that the Macedonian lifestyle is superior to that of the West is fiercely defended. There are also those who defiantly proclaim that they would never live anywhere else, citing the social life and close personal relationships that characterize life there. A pro-government professor gained notoriety in 2016 for attempting to lend academic credence to that notion by arguing that life in the West is lonely and difficult, with its 12-hour working days and lack of social contact. She characterized those who had left as unpatriotic turncoats and attempted to appeal to a sense of Macedonian nationalism in the hopes of keeping others from following suit. The article was widely circulated on social media within Macedonia, primarily because of her dubious claim that unrequited love, rather than financial difficulties or economic opportunity, is really what drives people to live abroad.

While her intent was to deflect criticism away from the embattled government for the country's low standard of living and her conclusions were soundly lampooned on social media, the article did touch on many of the same pieces of conventional wisdom that I heard so many times while I was there. Namely, that life in the West is harder than you think, that you will never get used to the "cold" lifestyle, and that Macedonia is a better place to raise a family because people appreciate relationships more. Pushing politics aside, there is some evidence that the lifestyle is attractive enough to a small but noticeable community of foreign nationals who have decided to move to Macedonia on a permanent basis. There are also many Macedonians with dual citizenship who have spent significant time in another country but have chosen to move back, despite being able to pack up and leave any time they wish.

Those competing drives, a simultaneous repulsion from the living conditions and an attraction to the lifestyle, are very much what characterize daily life in Macedonia. Sorting out how those two sentiments can exist in the same space at the same time became an obsession of mine, so much so that I decided to write a book about it. On the one hand, the exodus of young people is so acute that it affects virtually every family and is a routine topic of daily conversation. Of course, I personally contributed to that exodus when my wife and I decided to leave Macedonia and move back to the United States. On the other hand, the refrain "If you have money life in Macedonia is great" can also be heard on a daily basis. I still field questions about my decision to leave because my wife and I both had decent jobs, we owned two cars, and lived in a decent apartment. To some people, it is not clear what more we could possibly want.

If there were just one simple answer, the emigration crisis would have been solved already. Like most things involving social phenomena, the issue is complex and will take many years to resolve. In the absence of concrete answers, it occurred to me that in discussing the most common question I got while I was living there I could at least provide some clarity. That simple question, "So, what's it like in Macedonia?" is surprisingly useful. On a basic level, it satisfies the curiosity of people on both sides. People from the United States ask that because they literally have no idea and are interested, and people from Macedonia ask because they want to know what it's like for a foreigner in their country. On a higher level, it offers a window into what life is in like Europe's recently independent or post-socialist countries, 25 years into the so-called transition process. The experience of Macedonia also provides unique insights on the functioning (and failures) of stalwart Western institutions like capitalism and democracy in the developing world, and speaks to 21st century processes like globalization and international migration.

Before getting too far into the book, I feel a few caveats are in order, as talking about the Balkans is often (ok fine, always) a sensitive proposition. First, even as I type these words, I can hear versions of the following comments floating in the ether, ready to pounce: "Macedonia is not a real country! Check its official name in the United Nations!" Its cousin is also nearby, ready to add its two cents: "Kosovo is Serbia! It always has been and always will be!" I get it, names are political and have meanings that transcend basic language. Just the same, I will be referring to Macedonia and Kosovo as stand-alone entities and leave the name issues for someone else to sort out. Good luck to them, I'm sure they will be successful.

I'm also picking up on another commentary that goes something like this: "Typical CIA trying to destabilize Macedonia! Typical Soros-funded propaganda!" I am an unaffiliated former resident of Macedonia who thought the place was interesting enough to write about, but then of course I would say that! For what it's worth, I have no connection to the American government, to the Macedonian government, or to any other government for that matter, and I have nothing to do with Soros or any of his foundations. I am not claiming to speak for Macedonia or to represent its citizens. There are plenty of capable voices there who are in a far better position to do that than me. This book contains my reactions to personal experiences, and is only told from my perspective as an outsider.

I did, however, make a concerted effort to understand the people and society during my time there. I married into the local culture (literally) and lived there full-time for three years straight. I went out of my way to fully immerse myself in order to get a better sense of how the average person lives and thinks. In the process I managed to learn Macedonian language reasonably well, and I even became proficient at reading and writing in Cyrillic. I made a point to associate more with locals rather than with the small population of western foreigners who work with various embassies and NGOs. Doing so allowed me to amass a collection of anecdotes and observations about life in Macedonia, and to witness the personal lives of friends and family who live there, which then became the basis for this book.

Second, and perhaps more to the point, astute readers may note that what I refer to as my experience with "Macedonia" could more correctly be called my experience with Skopje. To be even more specific, my experience with Skopje could more correctly be referred to as my experience with the ethnic Macedonian part of Skopje. Critics could also point out that by implying my experience is representative of Macedonia as a whole, I am denying the rich multiculturalism that characterizes the society at large. Allow me to say that I am aware of those limitations, and want to acknowledge from the beginning that I understand the validity of those points. Skopje is not synonymous with Macedonia, and Macedonians are not the only group in the country. Albanians, Roma, Turks, Serbs, Bosnians, Vlachs, Jews, and many other groups have for many centuries been an essential part of what is now the Republic of Macedonia. Although I did work mostly with Albanians and Turks during my time there and still count them among my friends, nearly all of my social life outside of work was limited to the ethnic Macedonian part of Skopje.

With those caveats out of the way, I think it is safe to return to question at hand: So, what's it like in Macedonia? Well, I'm glad you asked…

CHAPTER 2
Europe's Obscure and Uncharted Frontier

Macedonia is located at the crossroads between many cultural worlds: East and West, Christianity and Islam, Europe and Asia, wealthy and developing. Throughout its history these competing forces have tugged at the country's identity, creating a complex mosaic of ethnicities, cultures, traditions, languages, and religions. Although it is geographically part of Europe, five centuries of Ottoman rule left a strong cultural imprint that is more akin to Turkey and the Middle East than to its Austro-Hungarian influenced neighbors to the northwest. For half of the 20th century it was administered as a socialist federal republic in Yugoslavia, leaving behind an institutional legacy that continues to influence its transition to democracy and free market capitalism more than 25 years later.

Trying to get to the bottom of all those tangled histories and identities is a fool's errand that I will leave aside. I am much more interested in the modern incarnation of the state that peacefully separated from Yugoslavia in 1991. Even though the country is immensely proud of its independence, the transition away from its status as a socialist republic has been tough. Approximately the size of Vermont, the country is impoverished, landlocked, mountainous, and isolated in a part of the world that relatively few people visit. Many of the other countries that were once part of communist Eastern Europe have joined the EU and the Schengen travel area. As a result, they are now far more integrated with the West and benefit from the open trade and free movement that come with it. Even fellow ex-Yugoslav republics Croatia and Slovenia are now part of the European Union and have substantially increased their international profiles since becoming independent. Macedonia, by contrast, remains on Europe's cultural, economic, and political periphery.

For a certain type of adventurous traveler, though, exploring Europe's obscure and uncharted frontier is a very exciting prospect. Macedonia is one of the few countries on the continent with no McDonalds, giving it the cultural cachet of an edgy neighborhood that has yet to be gentrified. Being there is sort of like listening to a band that no one has heard of yet, just as "traveling around the Balkans" has a grittier, more authentic ring to it than traveling the well-trodden paths of France or Germany. Tourists have started to come in greater numbers, albeit still small relative to the likes of nearby Greece and Croatia, and travel writers have started to take notice, lumping it in with neighboring Albania and Bulgaria as the next "hot" European travel destination. The New York Times even named Macedonia among its 52 places to go in 2015, along with far more mainstream destinations like Milan, Singapore, and Orlando.

Macedonia's place on that list is not without merit. Its small size makes the tremendous amount of ecological diversity it possesses very accessible, including pristine lakes and picturesque mountains that tower 8,000 feet above an extensive wine country. There is an abundance of history and artifacts to explore, ranging from the ancient Macedonian kingdom of Alexander the Great to the Romans, Byzantines, and Ottomans. The country is extremely safe and accommodating to foreigners, and the level of English is generally quite high among the younger generation.

Skopje, home to nearly half of the country's population, possesses a chaotic energy to it that is exciting and entertaining, especially for people coming from the far more reserved cultural environs of North America and northwestern Europe. On almost any day of the week there are dozens of packed kafanas (akin to a tavern) with live music played right at the table. People stand up and dance, singing in full voice, with their glasses raised, and they are generally quite happy to show a foreigner the ropes. Every evening the largest Ottoman-era bazaar outside of Istanbul comes alive as hundreds of people shuttle back and forth between the many bars, cafes, and restaurants. A night out on the town starts late and ends early the next morning, and for those coming from higher income countries, the prices can't be beat. Drinks at most places are less than two dollars, and a full meal with salads and appetizers is in the ten- to fifteen-dollar range.

An earthquake destroyed over 80 percent of the city in 1963, leaving Yugoslavia the task of rebuilding it. As such, the landscape has the unique quality of being simultaneously endearing and off-putting. Many of the buildings adhere to the brutalist style of architecture that was popular in socialist countries at that time. Rows of identical eight-story apartment towers with stark, empty courtyards have this brownish-gray wash to them and no exterior embellishments. On the outside they look like giant boxes covered in poured concrete that was left to dry on its own. Many have broken window frames, chipping paint, and holes on the otherwise featureless façade. When seen alongside the elegant churches and mosques, however, the drab socialist architecture has an alluring charm. Multiple tour groups of brutalism enthusiasts come to Skopje every year to see these relics of a bygone time.

There are, of course, more mundane aspects of Skopje that are subject to the same forces of globalization that shape life anywhere else. The city offers all the modern amenities one would expect to find, such as state of the art fitness centers, shopping malls, and cafes. American music, television, and movies are routine features of daily life, especially among the younger generation. Walking around a local grocery store it is common to hear modern country hits playing over the speakers, and there are live broadcasts of NCAA basketball and NFL games on cable television. Celebrations like Halloween and Valentine's Day, plus the Americanized versions of Saint Patrick's Day and Cinco de Mayo, are starting to catch on. There are Black Friday sales at the mall the day after Thanksgiving, despite the lack of, well, Thanksgiving. Skopje can be so accessible to foreigners, in fact, that it is entirely feasible to live there for many years and never have the need to learn the language or acquire any additional cultural proficiency. Indeed, there are many communities of expats from all over Europe and North America that do exactly that.

Those who do make an effort to venture out of that bubble of familiarity get to see what daily life is like for everyone else, and will find a different world entirely. This can be an eye-opening experience for some people because by western standards, Macedonia is a developing country. It is one of the poorest states in Europe and experiences most of the same problems that other developing countries face: low salaries, outdated infrastructure, weak institutions, rampant corruption, and a massive outmigration of young people who have grown discontent with their standard of living. To live there is to learn how to manage those hardships because there is no way around it.

By global standards, however, Macedonia is actually above average with respect to indicators of overall wellbeing such as life expectancy, educational attainment, and income per capita. That means very few people experience hunger the way they would in some Sub-Saharan African countries, and most people have access to adequate housing, healthcare, and other basic necessities. The living standard may be a little low compared to what most Americans are used to, but it is certainly above what a large proportion of the global population has to deal with. The middle class gets by on less than $6,000 a year, a shockingly low figure to most westerners, but relative to the cost of living it is enough to pay the bills, buy the groceries, and have an occasional meal out. Most people can also afford a car, even though it is entirely feasible to get around without one.

    Nevertheless, living on just a few hundred dollars a month does present some challenges, no matter the cost of living. Once you leave the Macedonian bubble where the prices mostly reflect the local income, 300 euros spend a lot quicker. There is no "poor country" discount when buying a plane ticket, for example, or when you need to replace your old computer. Those prices are the same for everybody, regardless of their country's standard of living. In addition, salaries for most people do not come on a reliable schedule. It is relatively common for a business to simply not make payroll for a few months, and with a chronic unemployment rate of over 30 percent, workers have little recourse. They simply must continue showing up at work and waiting for those magic numbers to appear in their bank accounts. Sometimes one month's salary must be stretched for two or three months, making it nearly impossible to plan ahead financially.

For all the financial difficulties and hardships that characterize daily life in Macedonia, people always find time for friendship and socializing. The local culture places a high value on "*drustvo*," meaning companionship, or what Americans might call hanging out. Even when people are hanging out with their *drustvo*, they are also likely to be talking on the phone to another set of companions; that's how much they enjoy being in touch. Many people from the West, and especially Americans, like to have compartmentalized friendships based around specific activities when they hang out. People might have friends in a running club, and a different set of friends on a recreational soccer team, and still another set of drinking buddies, but they probably do not hang out beyond the confines of those activities. Americans may even start to get anxious just sitting around for multiple hours in conversation without those activities as a backdrop.

In Macedonia, by contrast, it is common to get asked to "coffee" nearly every day, which is really just a code word for sitting around in extensive conversation and may or not involve coffee. This may sound like a mundane point, but it is hard to overemphasize the extent to which hosting guests for coffee or going to coffee at someone else's house is central to the culture.

Going "*na gosti*" (to be someone's guest) involves a whole song and dance that is completely natural to locals, but may take some getting used to for an outsider. To begin, it is customary, but not obligatory, to take off your shoes as you enter someone's residence. As soon as you start the motion to take off your shoes, it is also customary for the host to tell you that it's not necessary, but for you to continue doing it anyway, and for the host to then give you "*papuci*" (slippers). People are pretty insistent on wearing slippers around the house, primarily because carpet is rare and insulation is poor, so the floors are legitimately cold. More importantly, and more bizarrely, there is also a common view that illnesses come "from below," meaning from cold feet, and *papuci* are meant to protect against that eventuality. It is best to just go with it, because people are not too interested in hearing your views on how that is not very scientific. Culture can be a weird thing.

Once you negotiate the slippers and finally enter, you will notice that the host has laid out food on the table, even though you were only expecting coffee. Usually the food is limited to chips or cookies and maybe some cheese, but if you are a foreigner who is visiting for the first time there will likely be an impressive spread of meats and cheeses, plus enough beer, rakija, and wine for an entire wedding party. Local hosts will often spend more money than they actually have in an effort to leave a good impression. That custom can be awkward for people coming from a country where the average income is nearly ten times higher, but refusing the gesture outright is far more awkward.

Now, about that food and drink. This is not a self-serve kind of situation. You will be immediately asked what you want to drink, and if you don't say beer or wine or rakija, the host will ask you why not, and proceed to convince you to have one, just one, just a little. Without fail, that one drink will become five or six. Plus, the whole time you are drinking, your host will be looking at your drink's level. As for the food, you will be incessantly prodded to take more. When you refuse because you are physically unable to ingest more food, the host will insist that you are not getting more because you are embarrassed and will serve you anyway.

This type of hospitality can come across as aggressive to an unsuspecting foreigner, and showy gestures can easily get lost in translation, but it is rooted in the Balkan tradition of not accepting the first offer. When a host asks his or her guests if they would like something else and they say no, the host is expected to ask them again, and usually even a third time. The guest, for his or her part, is also expecting to be asked multiple times and does not want to appear too eager by accepting on the first insistence. The whole routine goes something like this:

"Here, have a piece of cake."

"No, I couldn't possibly eat any more I'm too full."

"But it's so good, you should try just a little."

"No really, I'm too full."

"Just a little piece. It's really, really good, you'll see. Just a little."

"Ok, I will try it."

The host then brings out a giant piece of cake, much larger than advertised, but does not take one.

The guest then asks, "You're not going to have a piece?"

"Oh no, I'm not hungry at all," as if that was a stupid question.

The guest will then take one or two bites of the cake, say it's delicious, and leave the rest. To a foreigner from a different culture, this can come across as wasting a perfectly fine piece of cake, or worse still as a sign that it was not very good. But in Balkan culture, the whole point of that interaction is about showing hospitality and going through the routine of insisting and refusing, not about the cake itself. Accepting food or drink and then leaving it allows the host to fulfill that social obligation, while also allowing the guest to play defense against being served anything additional.

When I first arrived in Macedonia I was unaware of these unwritten social rules and frequently felt overwhelmed by earnest pleas to eat and drink as much as I could. Any time I went somewhere my host would constantly look over at my glass to see how much I had left. As soon as it got to half full they would fill it up again without even asking me. Drawing from my own cultural background, where it is impolite to be wasteful by leaving something unfinished, I took that as a sign that I needed to continue drinking. The longer we sat somewhere, the more drinks kept coming, like a sinister conveyor belt that would never stop serving me. Eventually I learned to just leave my cup full if I did not want anything else, even if that went against my own principles.

In the reverse scenario, I dreaded having guests over at first because it seemed like so much work. I felt constant pressure to be refilling drinks and making sure that there was food on the table. Instead of having relaxed conversation with my company, I felt like a waiter that was on the verge of a major cultural faux pas if I accidentally overlooked a cup that was getting a little low. Macedonia also has one of the highest smoking rates in the world, and when people would come over they would just light up inside my apartment and expect me to have an ashtray ready. I hate cigarettes, and the smell would linger for days. Once the guests left, they would never even offer to pick up after themselves, leaving me to clean up all their dishes and put away all the food. If this is what it takes to have friends and earn respect, I thought, I will be happy to live a life of solitude.

Many westerners have a whole different set of routines and expectations regarding hosting guests. Whereas a Balkan guest will not even ask for a glass of water without being offered first, guests where I am from are expected to take what they want on their own. They may even get up and open the refrigerator, and then open the cabinet and get their own cup. When a guest from back home gets up and is ready to leave, the host obliges and shows them the door. People have jobs to wake up for and other things to do, after all, so it would be rude to try and prevent them from that. Leaving a Balkan home, by contrast, involves no small amount of haggling and repelling persistent offers to stay for just one more drink. This is true even if the host is obviously about to fall asleep and has nothing left to give. It's just considered polite to insist.

    Over the top hospitality is such an integral part of the culture that failure to follow the expected customs comes across as a sign of disrespect, which feeds into the rather pervasive stereotype that westerners are "cold people." Even I became guilty of that accusation when I experienced reverse culture shock upon returning to the United States after a long absence. I felt like I was watching a National Geographic documentary about myself as I was trying to rationalize that my American hosts were not being rude, they just have different ways of doing things. Still, every time I entered someone's house and they did not even get up from their chair to greet me or immediately bombard me with a drink selection, I couldn't help but feel like maybe we could learn a thing or two from Balkan hospitality.

But culture has a funny way of cutting both ways. For every interesting or positive aspect that I encountered, such as hospitality routines and the importance of *drustvo*, there are some things about Balkan culture that are more difficult to take. Jealousy, spite, and ill will towards success, for example, are deeply engrained sentiments that come to the surface quite often. I once heard a cliché that succinctly captures the character of this cultural aspect: In America if you build a new house, your neighbor will want to build a bigger one, but in Macedonia your neighbor will want to burn it down. There is some modicum of truth to that statement, in part because life's successes are so often the result of some injustice rather than hard work. If someone gets a new house or car, many people's first thought is likely to be "what crime did they get away with to get that?" Although an actual crime may not have been committed, the person probably did benefit from some form of injustice or favoritism. Getting ahead and acquiring new possessions through more honest or meritorious means is often considered too difficult to be realistic.

Spite and jealousy can take many forms, ranging from passive to outwardly hostile. The most passive form is gossip. People need something to talk about over all that coffee they are drinking, and they are more than happy to gobble up any rumors or conspiracies that may be floating around. Sometimes they are benign, even comical, like the time that someone told me with a great deal of conviction that President Obama is getting divorced because of his affair with Beyonce. Other times they can be more personal, like rumors that someone's daughter is sleeping around because she was seen out having coffee with another man. The person who started the rumor may be jealous that someone else's daughter seems to have a happy marriage and their daughter does not, or it may come from a spiteful intention to hurt someone for no good reason. To an outsider these sorts of actions are easy to ignore and laugh off, but in a society as social and family oriented as Macedonia, they can actually cause real damage in otherwise solid relationships.

Another mostly passive form of spite and jealousy is the use of black magic and witchcraft, which is widespread in the Balkans. The belief in mysticism is so pervasive that it is far more common to go to a fortune teller than to a psychologist to seek help with life's problems. Some people even go to healers who offer magic potions in addition to their medical professional. In the midst of a feud someone may leave black chicken feathers on her neighbor's doorstep, or privately ask a fortune teller to inflict some sort of bad luck on an adversary. When you are a firm believer in science, it can be hard to reason with someone who is worried that their crazy mother-in-law cast a spell on them. Nonetheless, this is a rather common occurrence, and is generally motivated by feelings of revenge, jealousy, ill will, or spite.

As innocuous as those forms spite and jealousy may be, the outwardly hostile forms can cause actual physical damage. A neighbor who does not really appreciate you walking your dog in the neighborhood, for example, may leave poison along your route for the dog to find. Stories of pets suddenly falling ill and dying shortly after are sadly common. Since I actually brought my dog with me when I moved, I had to get used to making sure he did not take an interest in anything he found on our walks out of fear that he would ingest something toxic. To this day it is not clear how a person could possibly feel good about intentionally killing another person's pet, but it happens more than I was ready to believe. On more than one occasion people would aggressively shout at us from their windows just for walking outside, threatening to come out and kill the dog if we did not get out of their sight. On another occasion an elderly lady actually threw rocks at us for passing on the sidewalk near her house, simply because she did not like seeing us.

    I understand that part of their spiteful hostility in that instance comes from a ubiquitous and irrational fear of dogs, but the source of that is not completely clear to me. It could be because parents often scare children into behaving by telling them that they will get "the dog" to bite them, so they instill fear at very early age. It could also be that there are packs of stray dogs who roam the city and can occasionally become aggressive, although in my experience they were more scared of me than I was of them because of all the abuse they had endured from people on the street.

The most likely reason, as far as I can tell, is related to the way in which self-conscious masculinity carries over into dog ownership. Tough guys must have tough-looking and potentially dangerous dogs. The bigger the dog, and the more aggressive demeanor it has, the more masculinity the owner exudes. If a Doberman or Rottweiler intimidates others, that is kind of the point. There is even a pervasive belief that it is good for male dogs to mate so they can feel good about themselves and build confidence. At vet clinics, bulletin boards are covered in hand written notes saying "I have a handsome dog looking to mate with a female." There are never, ever notes saying a female needs a mate or even that there are puppies available. Perhaps it goes without saying that neutering a dog is considered unreasonably cruel, even inhumane, which contributes in large part to the high population of stray and unwanted dogs. Neutering is an obvious and extreme threat to a dog's masculinity, and by extension, to that of his owner.

Racism and ethnocentrism are also widely tolerated forces in the culture, and in some cases they are even encouraged. Both of these social ills exist in the United States as well, but they manifest themselves in different ways. First, the prolonged trend towards political correctness in the United States has caused racism in particular to become far subtler. It most certainly still exists, but it is no longer socially acceptable to openly express those feelings. Political correctness is a rather new concept in Macedonia, and will likely take many more years to find a popular hearing. Using derogatory terms to identify an ethnic or racial group, directing monkey chants towards black players at sporting events, striking a karate pose and bowing to an Asian in the street, and otherwise discussing entire racial, ethnic, or religious groups through crude stereotypes are all common and perfectly acceptable behaviors. Very few people see harm in these actions, and mostly find them comical.

Second, in Macedonia there is no serious social conversation about addressing those issues, primarily because they are not even seen as issues to begin with. The idea that people can be placed into relatively uniform boxes is taken as a given, natural part of the world. Germans live in Germany and they speak German and they look and behave in a certain way, just like the French live in France where they speak French and look and behave in certain way. The notion that black and brown people simply cannot be a part of European society because they do not fit into those boxes is mostly unquestioned.

If you are foreign in Macedonia, one of the first things people want to know about you is "what you are," as in what ethnic or cultural box do you belong in. This is by no means subtle. People are very open about it. If you are a white person, they are very likely to ask you, "Are you one of ours," as in from the diaspora. If you are not, they will then try to place you into your correct category. Just that phrase "one of ours" is indicative how binary ethnic categories are in the Balkans. I was told many times about my Germanness, even though I have never been to Germany (except in an airport), do not speak a word of German, and have no relatives there.

Along the same lines, homosexuality does not fit into the rigid boxes that define society. Men should behave like stereotypical macho men and be attracted to women who behave like stereotypical obedient wives. Since homosexuality deviates from that norm there is a pervasive belief that it is a sort of mental illness, even among people who would otherwise be considered liberal. There are gay bars in Skopje, but they are as inconspicuous as possible because it can be dangerous, even deadly, to be out in the open. In 2014 the government looked the other way when a group of masked thugs smashed up a gay bar and beat some of the patrons with baseball bats. That was the sixth such attack in the space of two years, and as in the previous instances, there were no arrests and only a token investigation. Many people privately suggested that they were asking for it by gathering in public like that in the first place. Gay pride parades, unsurprisingly, are banned in Macedonia, just as they are in many Eastern European countries.

As I point out these downsides of the culture, I would be remiss to not emphasize that I am speaking in broad terms. Even though many of the tendencies and attitudes described have widespread support at the social and institutional levels, there are plenty of people in Macedonia who love dogs, strive for political correctness, and promote diversity and inclusion. Some of them do so at great personal risk. There is also an active protest culture that bravely struggles against social injustice, and the younger generation has a decidedly more cosmopolitan worldview than their predecessors. I am aware that cultural change, no matter where in the world, can be a slow-moving and incremental process, and that Macedonia is a new country that is still finding its feet when it comes to democracy. I could just as easily make a list of the many reprehensible aspects of my own culture, including institutional racism, dangerously extreme positions on guns, and rapidly rising inequality. That being said, my goal here is not to disparage, but rather to give a realistic and fair portrayal of what it's like in Macedonia, warts and all.

CHAPTER 3

Makedonska Rabota: Getting by in Daily Life

Prior to moving to Macedonia, I had already spent about half of my lifetime living apart from my parents. Out of necessity I learned how to cook, clean, do laundry, and pay the bills, just like most other people in my demographic group back home. If anything, I was a little behind my peers, as many of them had already purchased a house and started a family at that point. For a variety of reasons, that is just not how things are done in Macedonia. Perhaps the most important factor is that very few young people can afford to move out of their parents' residence and live on their own. For reasons that I cannot understand, the average rent in Skopje is approximately equal to the average monthly income, even though there are hundreds of empty apartments in the city that could use tenants. There is also a segment of the population who could possibly afford to move out but does not because of a latent stigma against renting, which I assume goes back to the days of Yugoslavia when pretty much everyone could afford to buy a house or apartment. And there are others still who just like having mom cook and clean for them and see no reason to change.

Because of all these factors, it is completely common and acceptable for grown children to live with their parents well into their 30s, and in some cases even longer. There are some exceptions of course, but nearly everyone I know has some sort of shared living arrangement that would be considered unconventional back in the United States. Most often the parents sleep in the living room and the two kids share the only bedroom. If there is a second bedroom, sometimes an aunt, uncle, or grandparent may live there as well. Compared to what most Americans are used to, living arrangements can be cramped and privacy hard to come by, but people make do with what they have.

    Just the same, I had not lived with my own parents since I was a teenager and had become used to a certain way of life, so living with someone else's parents in my thirties was simply not an option. By the time I moved there my wife had already secured us a 400 square-foot, one-bedroom apartment in a sturdy Yugoslav-era building where we could be on our own. When I say sturdy, I mean that the walls were giant, 12-inch thick concrete slabs. Many of the newer buildings, built as they are in a capitalist system that values profit above all else, are of noticeably lower quality. Unscrupulous construction firms scrap on building materials, fail to observe codes, and find any other way they can to save money. It is not uncommon to move into a brand new apartment and then to immediately have to replace all the fixtures and repaint the walls, and in some cases more serious repairs are required. As drab and bland as it looks, the singular purpose of socialist architecture was to allow people to live and work in what could reasonably pass for "modern" conditions at the time. The frills and luxuries and embellishments could be left to the decadent West.

I remember entering my building and looking at the dark, featureless hallway with exposed fuse boxes and wires and cracks in the walls. Even though the building was very much average for Skopje, and there were certainly many buildings in far worse condition, it looked and felt like a tenement. The grass around the building was overgrown and littered with wrappers and cigarette butts, the door frame at the entrance did not seem to fit the door so it was always open, and there was trash on the floor where people would just throw down their unwanted mail. As bad as the building looked from the outside, however, the apartment itself was mostly modern and clean on the inside. Many of the older buildings, in fact, follow that same pattern: old and dilapidated on the outside, renovated and modern on the inside. Paradoxically, many of the newer buildings are the opposite: renovated and modern on the outside, falling apart on the inside.

The biggest problem with older buildings is not their construction, but rather that they tend not to have central heating. They might have an old radiator, but that is centrally controlled by the state-run heating company and costs a surprising amount of money to turn on. A lot of people choose to keep the radiator off and either heat with a wood burning stove or with electric heaters. Older buildings also have ill-fitting windows that are no match for the winter winds and temperatures, which I suspect is one reason why people are so deathly afraid of "the draft" (*promaja*). Since I moved there in January, and we only had one heater in the living room, the temperature in the bedroom was only a few degrees warmer than outside. For the first two nights I insisted that we sleep in the regular bedroom like regular people, no matter how cold it was. By the third night, I realized that maybe it was best to start sleeping in the slightly warmer living room on the couch until it got warmer. I was Balkanizing, and it only took a few nights of winter to start.

  Apart from the sleeping situation, I soon learned that Macedonian bathrooms are also something to get used to if you are coming from the United States. If you want hot water, you have to plan ahead and turn on the boiler. For the uninitiated, a boiler is a small water heater mounted on the bathroom wall that you use on an as-needed basis. That means that if you like to take a hot shower first thing in the morning, you will need to plan that the night before. Another unique feature about the bathrooms is that they all have a drain in the middle of the floor. That's because for some reason shower curtains are something of a novelty, and it is just expected that when you take a shower, all that water on the floor is going to need somewhere to go. The bathroom also doubles as a laundry room and storage closet, so it can get pretty cramped in there.

By local standards, however, I was pretty fortunate. I was able to rent my own place, and more importantly I was able to find a decent job very shortly after I arrived. The demand for English language instruction is so high, especially from a living and breathing native speaker, that I did not need any connections or even a work permit to start teaching at a private language school. I worked evenings, 20 hours a week, and brought home 300 euros a month. At that rate my yearly income would work out to less than 5,000 dollars a year. Not bad for Skopje, especially considering that it was essentially a part-time job. There are many locals who would dream of having such an arrangement because money, or the lack thereof, weighs so heavily on their minds.

Once I started understanding the language better I came to realize just how often financial concerns come up in everyday discussions. Complaints and concerns about the standard of living, high unemployment, and financial instability are routine topics of daily conversation. In fact, one of the first Macedonian words I learned was "*katastrofa*," which is a common way to describe one's pay and general level of satisfaction at work.

I haven't been paid for the past three months. Katastrofa.

My boss cut our salary by ten percent for this month because we made a mistake. Katastrofa.

The car is broken again but I won't have any money to fix it for the rest of the month. Katastrofa.

But like many things in Macedonia, the average person's relationship with finances is fraught with contradictions. Despite constant gripes about not having money, it is often hard to find a seat at a coffee bar, and clubs are packed with people buying expensive drinks five nights a week. There are quite literally sports betting parlors on every block that are constantly busy, and every shopping center has a casino. Young people wear expensive name brand clothes and have the latest smartphones, and there is a surprising number of high-end German cars on the road. Regardless of their financial situation, many people view it is a given that they will take a two-week vacation to the beach every summer. Upon observing the apparent disconnect between financial means and spending behavior, many outsiders are left searching for an explanation.

Part of the reason is the cultural tendency to show and judge. Even though salaries are low for pretty much everyone, sitting at a high-end coffee place, paying for table service at a nightclub, and wearing clothes with the brand or logo prominently displayed confer a great deal of status. While this not unique to Macedonia, the pressure to appear well-off, and the judgment that people are subjected to when they do not, is much more intense and open than many westerners are used to. The aforementioned high-end German car is much more than a status symbol. It is signal to everyone else that the driver is not only above you on the social ladder, but also above the law. That sort of money is so hard to come by in the Balkans that one can only assume it was gotten through, shall we say, illicit means. Whether that is true or not (although it most probably is), they flaunt their showpieces for all to see by parking where and how they want and driving as fast and as recklessly as they want. I called them Audi-assholes.

Perhaps an even more extreme example of the social charade can be found in the villages, where oversized, western style mini mansions in various stages of completion sit in otherwise empty fields. They are the trophies of those who have left and now make money in the wealthy countries of the West. In many cases, the houses are either empty or only have a small number of finished rooms where those who remained behind actually live. The point is not necessarily to live large, but rather to give that impression to others.

Balkan social customs also ensure that there are far more occasions to display material wealth than in the West. There is an expression in Macedonian, *"treba da castis,"* which literally means "you should treat," as in pay for me. To most westerners this concept has no meaning, but *"castenje"* (treating) is an essential component of Macedonian and Balkan culture. At its most basic level, treating means that when someone marks a milestone in life, he or she is expected to publicly celebrate by passing out chocolates or some other sort of sweet to everyone at work or school. A broad range of milestones qualify, including getting a promotion or raise, obtaining a new job, or buying a new car or house. Even something as basic as getting one's salary could be reason enough to treat if the person chooses. Treating can also commemorate life's tragedies and hardships, such as the anniversary of a loved one's death, although the vast majority of occasions are positive.

In addition to treating at work or school, it is also customary to host parties to further commemorate life's bigger occasions such as birthdays, the birth of a child, name days, and feast days in honor of a particular saint (called a *slava*). Birthday parties and name day celebrations can vary in size, but either way the host is expected to pay for everyone's food and drinks. Rarer occasions, such as the birth of a child, call for even bigger celebrations. A day or two after a child is born, it is customary for the father to pay for everyone who attended the wedding to eat *mekici* (pronounced mek-eet-see) at a restaurant, which is a type of unsweetened fried dough. Served with the *mekici* is an all-you-can-eat assortment of cheese and salad, and of course plenty of booze. There is usually live traditional music, and once the rakija gets going, singing and dancing as well. One notable exception to the guest list is the mother, who sits alone at the hospital with the baby. The parents host and pay for a similar party a year later, this time with mom in attendance, to celebrate the child's first birthday, which is often preceded by a baptism. Each of these celebrations can easily run into the hundreds of dollars, which for most people in Macedonia is more than a month's salary. On more than one occasion I saw new parents begin to fret about the cost of their child's first birthday party shortly after leaving the hospital for the first time.

Hand in hand with the "treating" ritual is the judging ritual. At work or school, colleagues and classmates will begin assessing how much money the person spent on those chocolates as soon as they leave the room. At the bigger occasions like birthdays or *mekici*, they comment on how much food was on the table, how expensive it was, or the quality of the restaurant. At weddings people make comments about who brought what gift and how expensive the cake was. Although I never saw this in Skopje, it is customary in some rural villages throughout the Balkans to even announce who brought what gift over the microphone. The more lavish the celebration, the more satisfied the guests are, and the less the host runs the risk of being called cheap.

From the outside, this tendency seems counterproductive in a society where nearly everyone has low salaries and lives on a shoestring budget. One could correctly conclude that money could be better spent in other, more productive ways. From the local perspective, however, the custom of treating is a sign of respect and friendship governed by an unspoken system of social deposits and withdrawals. I may have to break the bank to host a birthday party or *mekici* celebration today, but doing so ensures that I will be invited to similar events in the future where I can eat and drink as much as I want for free. While no local would put it in those blunt terms, *castenje* is based on a social give and take that eventually balances out.

Life in Macedonia also entails learning how to negotiate the daily ordeals that are collectively referred to as "*Makedonska rabota.*" The expression literally means "Macedonian thing," but it can be better translated to "that's Macedonia for you." This can include a broad range of experiences, ranging from unpleasant inconveniences to blatant injustices that can make daily life a grind. Driving culture is perhaps the most obvious manifestation of *Makedonska rabota*. Compared to how friendly most people are in private company, they can become raging maniacs behind the wheel. As a general rule, the more expensive the car, the more careless and aggressive the driver. To be fair, the majority of the people drive normally. The problem is that the percentage of reckless drivers is high enough to create an unnecessarily chaotic environment that leads to multiple pedestrian deaths and car wrecks per year due to speeding, running red lights and stop signs, and driving while intoxicated. Even though there are sobriety checks, they are easily "taken care of" for the well-connected and wealthy. For everyone else, the penalties are minimal, involving a simple fine, even for repeat offenders.

Likewise, those who run over and kill pedestrians with their cars can use connections to avoid any criminal penalties whatsoever. For a country of less than two million people, car-related deaths occur with shocking frequency.

Under those conditions, driving can feel like more of a stressful competition than a means to an end, although it is not clear how anyone wins. An average car ride through Skopje consists of furiously honking the split second the light turns green, cutting in line, blocking the intersection instead of waiting for the next light, passing aggressively on two-lane residential streets, running through red lights, and cursing while gesturing wildly. If there is even a slight back up at a left turn light you can be sure that at least one person will simply go around the line of waiting cars and turn from the straight lane. Inevitably this leads to even more honking, wild gesturing, and in the end, more waiting. I liken driving there to playing a video game. You know something unexpected is going to happen at any moment, and if you want to advance, you have to negotiate that obstacle and prepare for the next one.

I learned not to leave any space between my car and the one in front of me to prevent getting cut off, and also to avoid driving in the right lane because of the high likelihood that the car in front of me would stop without warning and park right on the road. On more than one occasion I was forced off the road by a car speeding at me head on from the opposite direction. From what I could gather the driver did not feel like sitting in traffic in his lane and very cleverly decided to pass the line of cars by simply driving in my lane, all the while honking and flashing his lights as if it was my responsibility to get out of his way so he wouldn't hit me. I intentionally say "he" because such behavior almost always involves a he, despite the widespread perception that female drivers are the real problem. Even women generally hold the view that female drivers are inferior.

Those who have lived for some time in the West and have returned to Macedonia may use *"Makedonska rabota"* to describe the local manner of public behavior compared to that of Holland or the United States. For example, the process for something as simple as entering a concert or a sporting event generally involves delays, pushing, and cursing as everyone tries to get to the front of the line at the same time, which in turn makes the wait even longer. By contrast, one friend who came to visit me in the United States marveled at how patiently everyone sat in their cars, without even honking, as we were all waiting to enter the parking lot to see a tennis match featuring some of the world's top players. The same process in Skopje would have involved a cacophony of horns, aggressive gesturing, cutting off other cars, and definitely not waiting for directions from the parking attendant. Come to think of it, there would not be a parking attendant present in the first place. Likewise, if you take a direct flight from Skopje to Western Europe, you will notice that the moment the plane touches down on the runway people are already standing up and getting their luggage out of the overhead bins, ignoring the exasperated pleas from the flight crew over the loudspeaker. Patience, it turns out, is not a virtue.

By year two in Macedonia, I noticed that I had also adjusted what I had come to accept as normal public behavior. On a brief trip to Holland, where hundreds of people zip back and forth on their bikes amid the pedestrians and other street traffic, I saw two cyclists narrowly avoid crashing into each other. From my newly adopted Macedonian perspective I was prepared to see an epic argument complete with swearing and aggressive posturing, possibly even a physical confrontation, because in Macedonia it's always the other person's fault. Much to my surprise, the two cyclists smiled and simultaneously made the universal gesture for, "No, you go ahead." They then rode off in their respective directions, smiling and waving goodbye. The fact that such a banal expression of civility stood out to me at all is a testament to how sorely that is lacking in Macedonia.

Local explanations for this disparity in public behavior range from defensive to resigned. On the defensive side, there is a tendency to reason that people in Macedonia have a much harder life than people in the West and therefore are behaving in an understandable manner. People have a sour disposition because they are overworked, underpaid, and uncertain about the future. Westerners, it is assumed, would behave in the same way under those conditions. On the resigned side, people will openly discuss that there is a lack of "culture" in Macedonia and in the Balkans more generally. I was told many times by Macedonians themselves that Balkan people are uncivil by nature, bad seeds, and that nothing will ever change. In other words, *Makedonska rabota*.

The resigned viewpoint is in sharp contrast to the ubiquitous belief that life in Macedonia is qualitatively better than in the West, primarily because of the strongly held perception that westerners do not know how to enjoy life. On a certain level, I understand where this is statement is coming from. Life in the West, and especially in the United States, can be so career focused that it can significantly take away from family and leisure time, both of which are highly valued in Macedonia. The ultimate symbol of our collective failure to properly enjoy life is the drive-thru window at Starbucks, which borders on sacrilege to Balkan people who are accustomed to drinking their coffee with friends and colleagues on extended breaks throughout the day, including during working hours. When Macedonians go to live abroad, they often complain about the lack of social time and find westerners to be standoffish and reserved. They take those cultural differences as signs that the people in their adopted country are somehow unhappy with life or that they do not know how to "enjoy."

While it is certainly true that the average American has to

be reminded to take time to stop and smell the roses, I found the idea that the Balkan lifestyle is somehow more enjoyable to be problematic for at least two reasons. First, how could one possibly quantify what is more enjoyable? I get quite bored, for example, sitting for a two-hour coffee and talking incessantly, even though many of my Macedonian friends and family find that to be highly enjoyable. We just enjoy different things, and that is not inherently better or worse. Second, once I started to understand the language, I began to strongly question what the average person is actually enjoying. Typical conversation is characterized by crushing negativity, and there is endless complaining about the unpleasantness of accomplishing basic daily routines like driving and standing in line at the grocery. Life may be more oriented around work and time in the West, but utter lack of patience and an irrational hurry to get somewhere as fast as possible and at any cost can make life in Macedonia far more tense and stressful than it needs to be.

    The expression *Makedonska rabota* can also refer to the shear amount of time and effort it takes to get even basic errands done. There is still widespread distrust of online banking and payments, causing interminably long lines at any institution for which a monthly bill is due. Paying the phone bill and then stopping at the bank to deposit a check could take multiple hours. Attempting to get anything done at a government institution is far more daunting, as I learned during my quest to secure my first residential permit in 2013. I alluded previously to the frustrating runaround I got on the phone, but that was nothing compared to what transpired after I was actually there. Since I was married to a citizen, and Macedonia is not a prime immigrant destination, I naively assumed that getting a residential permit would be a matter of signing a few papers, paying a few fees, and going on my way. I was told on the phone, after all, that it really was not a big deal and that I should not bother trying to set it up ahead of time because it was so straightforward. Instead, it turned out to be a weeks-long saga that was arduous even by Eastern European bureaucratic standards.

The process began with a trip to the 9th floor of the MTV building (Macedonian Television and Radio), which involved taking a 40-year old elevator of very suspicious quality with enough space for four, but seven people still crammed their way in. Once the doors closed, the overhead light didn't work, and the buttons didn't have lights either, leaving me in the uncomfortable position of being in a small, pitch black box with a bunch of strangers of varying hygienic practices. It does not help that many of the older people eat onions and garlic like there is no tomorrow, and smoke at least a pack a day. That combination of smells in a small enclosed space is, how to put it diplomatically, unpleasant.

When the doors opened to the 9th floor, I was confronted

with a typical feature of Macedonian bureaucracy: long hallways of closed, unmarked doors. Since I did not already know where I was going, my only option was to find a door that wasn't locked, open it, poke my head in, and ask the annoyed office worker if I was in the right place. A big reason why the office worker was annoyed was because 15 other people before me had done the same thing and asked the same question. One might ask, "Couldn't this problem be solved by, say, having a receptionist direct people or by at least having informative signs on the doors?" To which I would say, "Yes. Yes it could."

For a building that performs essential government functions, it was in a surprising state of disrepair. There were water stains on the ceiling, stains and holes all over the well-worn carpet, broken windows patched with duct tape, and cracks in the walls. Even though there was the universal "no smoking" symbol posted in the otherwise featureless hallway, clouds of cigarette smoke wafted from underneath some of the closed doors. When I finally found a sign taped to a door, it said that they only work with foreigners on Tuesdays and Thursdays between the hours of 9 and 12. Fair enough, I thought, I will just get an application for a residential permit, fill it out, and bring it back on Tuesday at 9 in the morning.

When I returned on Tuesday at 9 with a completed application in hand, there was a near solid mass of people crowding the narrow hallway. I soon learned that there are no "lines," you just stand as close as you can to the front and peak your head through the door when it opens and hope for the best. I call this "zombie mode," because that's the best way to describe the sight of dozens of people pressing up against a door and hungrily trying to get in the second it opens. After finally making my way to the front, I was told to come back because I didn't have a translated and notarized copy of my passport, birth certificate, and criminal background check. It is hard to understate the importance that Balkan bureaucracies assign to official stamps and notaries. I ordered copies from America, and when they came I took a trip to the translator and then a trip to the notary to verify that my translation was official. Between paying for translations, notary stamps, copies, background checks, and postage, the costs were getting into the hundreds of dollars, and the days were turning into weeks.

With all the proper documents in hand, I went back to the 9th floor during the designated time and waded through another unorganized mass of people. Once again, however, my application was incomplete because I only produced a criminal background check for the last place I lived, Tennessee, and not for the United States. I tried to explain that each state has its own legal system and that I had lived in multiple states, but they kept insisting that there had to be some sort of background check from the United States government. So I ordered a background check from the FBI, waited for that to arrive, got it translated, notarized, and then went back to the 9th floor for a third time. Finally, I was able to drop off my application for it to be reviewed, but I would have to come back another day to see if it was approved.

Once the visa was approved, there was no message or email or phone call to notify me. I just had to take the elevator to the 9th floor on Tuesdays or Thursdays between 9 and 12, poke my head in various doors, and try my luck. Each time an exasperated office worker had to manually rifle through the paper files to try and find my name in the stack of approved visas. On the day mine was finally ready, I could see the applicants' country of origin on each of them as she searched: Kosovo, Kosovo, Kosovo, Turkey, Kosovo, Serbia, Turkey, United States… She pulled my file and then looked kind of annoyed. "United States? What are you doing trying to live in this miserable country?" she asked me. I answered with a nervous laughter, and she shook her head and let out a disappointed sigh at my poor life choice.

I was told to go wait in yet another chaotic mass of people to get my picture taken for my new "*licna karta*," or personal ID card. That process once again involved standing in the narrow hallway right next to the 9th floor elevator and trying to hear my name being called when it was my turn to enter. It is not an exaggeration to say the meat counter at the grocery store has a better way of dealing with lines than the government's immigration office. At the grocery, you take a number from a little machine, and when it's your turn the number pops up on a digital screen. At the immigration office, a woman sits at her desk and just reads out the name of the next person in a normal voice to a noisy mass of people on the other side of a closed door. If the person closest to the door is able to hear and is feeling helpful, they will shout the name they heard to the others. If not, you miss your turn.

After waiting about 45 minutes, my name was finally called, and I crowdsurfed my way to the photo room. The two ladies in the room didn't even acknowledge my presence and just continued talking amongst themselves. As I was waiting for instructions, one of them got up and started to walk out the door I had just entered.

"Where I should sit for my photo?" I asked.

"When am I supposed to drink coffee?!?" she shot back and left the room.

To put this situation in other terms, this is an office that deals with foreigners for three hours a day, two days a week, in a small country that is losing population and should be happy to have immigrants. During that window of time, they find it necessary to take coffee breaks, because when else should they drink coffee?

After a few minutes of awkwardly standing around, the other woman in the room motioned for me sit, snapped my photo, and told me to come back in a few months to pick up my new ID because the government currently did not have any plastic to print them. Instead I got a little piece of paper that served as my temporary ID. I could have made it myself. When I returned to pick up my real *licna karta*, I waited in another unorganized, chaotic mass, only this time in a different room. On the other side of the mass was a counter where we could presumably trade in the pieces of paper for a new ID. Propped up on the counter was a hand-written note on a piece of torn cardboard that read "ПАУЗА" (*pauza*), to indicate that the one worker responsible for passing out new IDs was on break. "Makedonska rabota," sighed one of the other people waiting in front me. Makedonska rabota, indeed.

Living in Macedonia on a full-time basis, it is hard to recognize how the process of mentally coping with these frustrations can wear on a person, or at least that was the case in my experience. I got used to these daily struggles, and any time I came back to the United States it felt weird to adjust to what used to be so normal. At intersections I started to pay attention to how people were *not* honking at me the second the light turned green to go. I noticed how friendly and smiley the customer service was, even at places like Wal-Mart where the average salary is probably comparable to similar establishments in Macedonia once you adjust for the cost of living. Perhaps more than anything, I was stunned to realize what passes for normal daily conversation. Back in Macedonia, where the hardships are legitimate and extensive, I felt suffocated by the constant complaints about politics and money and horror stories from work and all of the limitations on life. The normalcy of discussing topics like sports without arguing or even just the weather felt simultaneously comfortable and weird.

I also became acutely aware of being able to accomplish routine tasks in the space of minutes instead of hours, or even days, and without the help of an extensive network of "connections." For example, when I went to the bank back home, a smiling teller was immediately there to greet me with a "Hello! How may I help you?" I explained that my wife is not an American citizen, but that I would like to add her as an authorized user to my bank account. The teller took all the necessary information, and in a matter of minutes, we were on our way. As mundane as this experience was, it was immensely satisfying.

By way of comparison, I had opened a Macedonian bank account a few months prior. I waited in the usual unorganized mass of people, and when I finally got to the front of the mass I was dismissively told that I had been in the wrong place that whole time. I then waited in another unorganized mass of people, and when my turn at the teller came I was flanked by two complete strangers on either side who just thought it would be interesting to see all of my personal financial information and identification. The whole process took around 90 minutes. Subsequent trips to the bank rarely took less than 45 minutes and routinely involved speaking with multiple unfriendly and unknowledgeable tellers before someone could actually help me.

In fairness, I completely recognize that comparing Macedonia and the United States falls into the apples and oranges category, at best. Furthermore, life settled down quite a bit once I learned how to navigate the system a little better. I still dreaded the yearly process of getting my residential permit renewed, but the later trips were not nearly as difficult as the first. One reason things got easier, it must be pointed out, was because I developed a few connections of my own that made sure I was taken care of. Another, more important reason was because I found a way to accept my new normal and not be bothered by all the little inconveniences.

Acceptance was a slow process because when I first moved there all of the hardships were more of a curiosity than a bother. I felt like I was on an adventure rather than in a new home. As soon as I landed back in Skopje after my first trip to the United States, that new reality punched me in the face, and everything about the people and the place bothered me. All of the things that I thought were quirky or charming or interesting before started to be annoying. I became testy at the way people don't respect lines and drive like theirs is the only car on the road. I started focusing on how everything was so old and small and out of date, like the plumbing in our bathroom and our tiny refrigerator that didn't keep things cold if it was really hot outside.

Our apartment didn't have air-conditioning, but if I tried to open a window to cool off a little, people would ask me to close it because of the "breeze," which I was surprised to learn has the power to make you sick no matter how hot it is. This fear of the breeze was all the more annoying considering that so many people have no problem smoking a pack of cigarettes every day and drinking hard liquor at 10 in the morning. I started speaking and understanding the language better, but even that was annoying because it meant I had to listen to all the comments about even basic things that I was doing.

"Why did you put your shoes there? You will make the floor dirty."

"Ooooh, you've got the boiler on again? You turn it on all the time. That's expensive."

"Why did you pay that price for cucumbers? You could have gotten them for five cents cheaper at this other, much less convenient market."

If you're silently laughing to yourself right now, you probably have been to the Balkans or have relatives from there and can relate. I just couldn't understand why anyone cared enough to comment on anything I did, must less on the insignificant minutiae of my day. In order to survive, I had to make some adjustments. I started surrounding myself with as many modern material comforts as possible. I bought a new refrigerator that could keep my food cold even in the summer. I bought a car that didn't make me feel like I was driving a toy and didn't run the risk of breaking down unexpectedly. I bought a new bed with a mattress that was less than 30 years old, and kitchen appliances, and a drier. I also started going out of my way to find American friends, even though I had been trying to avoid hanging out with any up to that point. My Macedonian friends have been extremely accepting and patient with me, but when you're away from home and living with another language, it's comforting to get the depth in a conversation that comes from a shared background.

I now realize that my first year in Macedonia was a textbook example of the five phases of grief. This is not to say that I was depressed or grieving about living in Skopje. As I will discuss throughout this book, there are many wonderful aspects to life there, and in a short time I made far more friends in Macedonia than I have ever made in the United States. There are upsides and downsides to living in Skopje, just like there are anywhere else. Instead, I needed to pass through the stages of grief to allow my old mentality to die and to accept a completely new one that was more appropriate for my life as an expat in a very different culture.

During the first phase, denial, I did not mentally accept

the idea that Macedonia was my new home. When I first got there it was more of an extended stay in my mind, something like going away to school for a semester. The anger phase hit when I came back after spending the summer in America and realized that it wasn't temporary. I was not at all sure if I was up for the task of getting a new residential permit, or dealing with the driving culture, or learning a new language. Surrounding myself with modern material comforts and American friends was my way of trying to regain control of a difficult situation, also known as bargaining. Depression follows bargaining, which is a road well-traveled for many people living away from home. Missing holidays, birthdays, and weddings is no small matter, although modern technology does help alleviate the pain of homesickness to some extent. After a full two years of living there, I managed to reach the final stage of the adjustment process: acceptance. Acceptance of the culture, acceptance of the lifestyle, and most of all, acceptance of a new way of looking at the world.

CHAPTER 4
Celebrating Life, Celebrating Family

As part of Yugoslavia, Macedonians were united with Slovenes, Croats, Serbs, Bosnians, Montenegrins, Albanians, Roma, Turks, Vlachs, and many other groups under one flag. Orthodox Christians, Catholics, and Muslims were asked to set aside their ethnic and religious identities in favor of a Yugoslav one. Under the leadership of Tito, it mostly worked. The state did not ban religion outright, but it was pushed aside in favor of an identity and culture that would edify the state and its communist philosophy rather than a deity. Organizations like the Socialist Youth Union of Yugoslavia, for example, inculcated children with social values and gave them a sense of membership in a shared community; much the way being a member of a religious organization can do. Nearly every person born in Yugoslavia prior to 1983 remembers going through an induction ceremony to become one of Tito's Pioneers, and they may even still have photos wearing a red scarf and being presented with a red booklet that resembled a Communist Party membership card.

State-sanctioned rituals of that sort largely took the place of those associated with major religious observances, which were tolerated to some extent but were not official state holidays. Soldiers and government officials actively avoided religious displays and rituals altogether, and mosques and churches were closely supervised by those friendly with the state. Many communist governments throughout Eastern Europe, including that of Yugoslavia, designated New Year's Day as the period of holiday festivities since it is a neutral day unaffiliated with any religious calendar. They even borrowed from western Christmas traditions to inject a little holiday spirit into the celebration. Santa Clause (known as Grandfather Ice, which is awesome) still comes the night of December 31st and leaves presents under a New Year tree decorated with lights and ornaments. The only other holidays that the state recognized were Labor Day (May 1st), Republic Day, and a day honoring the military.

Now that Macedonia is independent, the country has undertaken a concerted effort to restore portions of its unique cultural legacy and to establish a post-independence identity. Orthodox Christianity has become an integral part of those efforts, but mostly as marker of nationality rather than as a philosophical or even moral construct. Among younger Macedonians, for example, it has become fashionable to wear prayer bracelets and cross necklaces, and they may talk openly about how they fast on Fridays and during Lent. Beyond that, they are not very likely to know even basic things about religious doctrine. Having grown up in (and survived) the Bible Belt, where it was common to go to church as many as three times a week and to attend Sunday school and Bible camps, it was amusing to me that so many people would proudly self-identify as Orthodox Christians but could not name even one of the four gospels. Incidentally, I totally rule the Bible categories on Jeopardy.

Hand in hand with the rise in religious self-identification is a growing interest in rediscovering the traditional celebrations that were suppressed during the communist time, especially those associated with religious holidays. That can be interesting to observe because the traditional customs and rituals fell out of practice during Yugoslavia, so many of them are as unfamiliar to a local as they would be to an outsider who is seeing them for the first time. Priests offer step-by-step instructions to help people navigate the proceedings because most of the revelers are rather unsure of what they are supposed to do or how they are supposed to be behave. The Easter service, for example, mostly consists of standing outside of the church in relaxed conversation and smoking cigarettes until midnight, at which time people break hard boiled eggs, eat them, and then the young people go to the club. Even when the priest comes out to address the crowd and offer the Easter sermon most people cannot be bothered to pay attention. There is, of course, a more formal aspect to the whole service, it's just that the vast majority of those in attendance are unaware of those other aspects and are largely uninterested to find out more. Likewise, on Christmas it is customary to stop by the church, tell the priest your name, enter for a few moments, and light a candle, but that's about the extent of the religious component. People celebrate the holidays, and they tend to have some awareness of their religious significance, but the church and the clergy play a mostly marginal role.

Apart from holidays, weddings are another rare occasion on which Macedonians venture into the church, but again the religious aspect is mostly tangential. The church portion of my Macedonian wedding, for example, comprised about ten minutes of a nearly all-day party. One reason for that is because in Skopje each church performs dozens of weddings on the weekends throughout the summer, so the length of the actual ceremony is cut down in order to meet the demand. In the winter months a wedding may last longer because there are fewer ceremonies booked. But ours was in late May, and when our caravan showed up at the church, another wedding party was about to enter, the previous wedding party was exiting, and we were next on the conveyor belt. Likewise, when our ceremony ended, we could hear the priests starting to sing as they entered with the next wedding party. In, out, next. By contrast, the church ceremony is a rather large component of many Southern Baptist-type weddings that I have attended. It may last an hour or more, and there is heavy emphasis on the "holy" part of matrimony. The reception usually only lasts an hour or two, not much more, and the whole event is wrapped up by the early evening.

Macedonians would no doubt scoff incredulously at such a meager wedding celebration. I was not exaggerating when I said that my wedding there lasted almost all day, and mine was small by local standards because very few people on my side were able to make the trip over there. Although not everyone follows traditional wedding customs, and there are variations on how they are practiced throughout the country, Macedonian weddings are way more interesting and much more entertaining that anything I have experienced in the United States. Many of the customs pertaining to wedding celebrations are adaptations of those from the Ottoman time, but these days people put a modern spin on them and incorporate them in their own ways.

In my case, we chose to follow the custom of the bride and groom hosting separate parties at their respective parents' residences early in the day. Since my parents live back in Kentucky, I had people come to the apartment we were renting, and she had people go to her mother's house just outside of the city. My party started at about one in the afternoon when musicians playing traditional music showed up to my apartment. We moved the furniture and danced the traditional "*oro*" right in the living room, and the entire building knew that there was a wedding party afoot. The *oro*, I should clarify, is a sort of circle dance in which everyone joins hands and, well, moves in a circle. Personally I am very grateful for the *oro* because its most basic form is easy for pretty much everyone to participate in without looking stupid. You join hands with the people next to you, take a few steps to the right, kick your left foot out, kick your right foot out, and continue. There are more complicated variations that actually require real skill and practice, but the basic form comprises about 90 percent of the dancing at most weddings. All the while, the booze flows like wine.

After an hour or two, we caravanned on over to the bride's hangout to continue the party. Once we got there, the musicians continued playing in front of the house, and my side did a circle dance in the yard before entering. When we entered we greeted her family, and did a few more circle dances in the living room. During that time the bride was still closed in a separate room with her closest female friends and younger relatives, while her male relatives symbolically guarded the door. To get to her, I had to negotiate a price with the guards, which is a previously agreed upon amount of money. The whole routine is a leftover custom from a bygone time when there were real prices and dowries to be paid for the bride. In modern times it is a fun charade that goes something like this: the groom offers the guards a certain amount of money, they say it's not enough, and the groom tries to push his way through anyway to break down the door. Repelled by the guards, the groom offers slightly more money, which is again refused for not being enough, and he tries to barge his way past the guards once more, unsuccessfully. He bargains a third time, the guards say the offer is getting better but still not enough, the groom tries to push his way through, and this time is able to enter the bride's chambers.

Once in the chambers together, the *dever*, one of my unmarried male friends, brought the bride's shoes and attempted to place them on her feet. As per the custom, she told him that the shoe did not fit quite right on the first attempt, so he placed some money in the shoe and tried again. Still she told him the shoe did not quite fit, and he placed a little more money and tried again. On the third try, she finally gave her approval and the shoe magically fit. After a few photos we left the bride's chambers together and performed a few more circles of the *oro* with the rest of the wedding party. Finally, before leaving the bride's residence to head out to the church, the two fathers of the couple ceremoniously spun a round loaf of bread three times and broke it into pieces for everyone to partake. As you may have noticed, the number three is kind of important in Macedonian customs. I am assuming that is because of its relationship to the Holy Trinity, although no one ever stated that explicitly.

By the time showed up at the church, the music and dancing and drinking had been going strong for many hours, and it was not even five in the afternoon yet. After the aforementioned ten-minute ceremony at the church, we moved the wedding party to a restaurant in a caravan of cars all honking with streaming dangling off the sides. The restaurant is really what most Macedonians associate with a wedding, because that is the only portion of the whole proceedings that most people attend. When someone says they are getting married, the first question people ask is inevitably "which restaurant," because that is where most people catch up to the party. The bride and groom pay for everyone to have a full meal and an open bar, and there is no shortage of circle dancing.

The biggest difference in dancing the *oro* at the restaurant as compared to earlier in the day is that the circle usually grows to over a hundred people as all of the newly arrived guests join in the fun. When that gets too unwieldy, a second and even third concentric circle forms around that. If you let yourself go and get into the moment, moving slowly around in a circle while holding hands with two strangers is a lot more fun than it might sound. In another contrast to most American weddings, pretty much everyone actually takes part in the festivities at a Macedonian wedding. The music goes non-stop until one in the morning, and the party stays strong the whole time because no self-respecting Macedonian would ever take off early. There are no cultural hang ups about openly celebrating or drinking like there are where I am from, and the atmosphere is very celebratory and festive.

As different as most of the wedding traditions are in Macedonia, some American customs have been adopted from what people have observed on movies and television shows.

Near the end of the evening, for example, the bride tosses a bouquet of flowers over her shoulder to a group of unmarried women and girls while the song "Single Ladies" plays in the background, and then the groom tosses the garter belt into a group of unmarried young men, although minus the Beyonce. Afterwards many of the young people stay out on the floor and dance to modern music from both the United States and ex-Yugoslavia. For the most part, however, the average Macedonian wedding experience is different and unique in a way that is far more exciting than its American counterpart. Better still, Macedonian weddings are way less stressful to plan, much easier to organize, and cost about ten percent of the average wedding in the United States.

    Shortly after the wedding come the incessant questions about when the couple will have children. This is not really seen as a choice, no matter what sort of financial situation or living arrangement the couple currently has, although having more than two kids would be considered unusual. Unlike in the United States, where parents are mostly left to raise their children on their own, having a child in Macedonia is a whole family affair that includes aunts, uncles, cousins, and of course the grandparents. The idea of hiring a babysitter simply does not exist because there is always at least one relative who would be happy to perform the task for free.

    Even though I did not yet have children when I lived

there, I also noticed that the society is much more kid-friendly than in the United States. There is less anguish about taking the kids in public, including to bars or restaurants, because people are generally more welcoming to the idea of a kid being around. Whereas in the United States the idea of "free range parenting" is considered novel, that is just normal in Macedonia. The country is incredibly safe, and there are always people out and about, so kids are free to go play outside and run around the neighborhood without their parents' immediate supervision.

At the same time, that means that there are also plenty of people ready to jump in and get overly stressed about minute things like whether or not the baby constantly has on socks. The slightest indication of a runny nose or just a fall in the course of play will send people into a near panic and generate a trip to the doctor. And then there are the many pseudo-scientific folk beliefs that are taken rather seriously by large proportion of people. These include things like the idea that the breeze (*promaja*) makes babies sick, or that walking barefoot causes illness, or that the air conditioning is somehow a vector for any number of maladies. Interestingly, they have no problem smoking around children in closed spaces, including right next to a baby's face while they are being held.

There are also many who believe that if a couple has had a baby in the past year, or if they were married in the past year, they should not attend a funeral or any sort of memorial service for the dead. Not only that, if someone did attend the service, that person should avoid contact with the couple until the next day. And telling someone you went to a fortune teller or some other kind of mystical intercessor is not laughed off as being ridiculous. For someone who is a big fan of logic and scientific reason, these beliefs were as interesting as they were infuriating.

Of all the different folk beliefs that I encountered, the one I found the most interesting was the belief that a baby should not leave the house until it is 40 days old. I had never heard of this practice, and when I asked people for an explanation, it went something like this:

"Why can't the baby leave the house for 40 days?"

"It's the 40 days."

"What 40 days?"

"THE 40 days. They just need to pass so that the baby can start going out."

"But what will happen if you go out before the 40 days?"

"The baby's immunity is too weak and it will get sick. It's not good to out."

For me, 40 days seemed like a rather specific time frame for an immunity system to universally develop. Why not 38 days or 43 days? Does every baby have the same immune system that develops in exactly the same way? Since we don't follow this practice in the United States, was it just pure luck that our population surpassed 320 million recently? After a quick Google search I found that the 40 days practice is actually a tradition rooted in the church; Jesus himself was blessed at the temple 40 days after his birth. Even though some parents take their baby to three houses and visit the church on the 40th day, communist secularization and modernization efforts throughout the 20th century have pushed the religious aspect of that practice aside and introduced a sort of pseudo-scientific legitimacy. Saying that it is good for the baby's immune system certainly sounds more logical that saying it is because of an ancient religious practice. Regardless of the explanation, knowledge of "the 40 days" is widespread in Macedonia. These days, however, many of the younger couples in Skopje are foregoing the tradition. If the baby seems healthy and the weather is tolerable, younger couples will take them out as soon as they feel ready, although not without ample protests from grandmothers, aunts, and any other older ladies who happen to be in the vicinity.

    Another cultural difference concerning children and family that I encountered, but was unprepared for, was the extent to which people value sons over daughters. It's not that people don't love their daughters if they have one, but they will openly and candidly tell you how much they hope to have a son instead. While I was there I saw pregnant women openly fret about the prospect of having a girl because their husbands were putting so much pressure on them to have a boy. How exactly that works is still a mystery to me, but I did get the strong impression that the woman was somehow responsible for the gender of the baby. In other instances, I know of men who went to psychological counseling so that they could come to accept the prospect of having a daughter. On the occasion that a son is born, his male relatives will talk with surprising frequency about the size of his, well, you know. The comments were so frequent and the jokes seemed so rehearsed, I got the impression that grown men sat around all day and tried to come up with the best one-liners about the exploits of the baby's giant manhood. It was, shall we say, unusual to experience.

As children grow up, parents expect to have a far bigger role in their lives and for a much longer time than most Americans are used to. They may demand to have a say in decisions about naming babies, or where their grown children should live, or who the godfather will be in their wedding. Independence among children, even if they are grown, is not considered a virtue, especially if the child is a boy. Mom does the laundry, cleans, cooks, irons, and washes the dishes until she physically cannot, at which point the daughter-in-law will likely take over. The idea that a son would do those things rarely comes up. Seeing grown men so dependent on their mothers while at the same time presenting as so macho was an incongruent image to me. Small children do not know how to do laundry, but a grown-up, man or woman, should have some ability to accomplish basic domestic tasks independently of mom. That is, at least, how I see the world.

That co-dependency is reinforced by the cultural expectation that parents are responsible for providing their children with property and a place to live. If a family has a house, for example, it is understood that a portion of that house will pass on to a child and that he or she will continue living there, usually upstairs from the parents. If the house has a yard that is big enough, then the parents will build a second house in the yard for their child. This cultural tradition has managed to persist into the 21st century, even if the economic reality is now such that many parents cannot afford to pass any property on to their children. The fact that Americans tend to have big empty yards and that their children tend to move out permanently at a young age instead of living rent-free with their parents strongly contributes to the notion that we are a cold and unloving people. Most people in Macedonia will spend their entire life in the same house or apartment, and that property will stay in the family once they are gone. Plus, credit is so hard to come by and real estate deals can be so corrupt that the average person does not have the option to acquire new property to begin with. That is in sharp contrast with the American practice of taking out a mortgage and moving from one house to the next or even one state to the next in pursuit of a better job or improved living circumstances.

Time and again I had to address this topic because my

parents have a large house with many bedrooms and big exurban yard, but none of their five grown children even live in the same state as them, much less in the same house. I had one colleague who very indignantly asked me why my parents were making me work and pay rent in such a poor country like Macedonia instead of allowing me to live with them in luxury. If his family had those circumstances, that is absolutely what they would have done, so he just could not imagine a valid reason why we would do things any differently. When I explained that our culture was different, that we value independence and making our own money and buying our own house, and that my parents probably did not particularly want a grown child and his wife living with them, he responded very earnestly, "Why doesn't your family love each other?"

    Family, as you may have gathered by now, is a much stronger bond in Balkan society than in the West. While there are many positive aspects to that, including many different types of support services that Americans would otherwise have to pay for, there can also be adverse effects on the society at large. When an uncle who works in the police takes care of his nephew's drunk driving ticket, or a cousin who works in a school changes a failing grade into a passing one, the result is that people learn to avoid the consequences of their actions. People run red lights and park wherever they want because they know that they can get it taken care of, even as they complain about how other people do the same thing when it does not benefit them. The person receiving the favor from the family member benefits in the short term, but it comes at the expense of social development at large. The United States, to be sure, has its fair share of nepotism, that is not in dispute. The Ivy League model, for example, is largely based on maintaining a closed society that is accessible through nepotism. The difference is that outside of the elites, the average person can go about daily life with nepotism being only a small concern. In Macedonia, it is the only concern.

      That being said, there are many lessons to be learned from the Balkan approach to family ties. Having closer families increases the sense of social support at all stages of life. Children always have someone nearby, even if their parents both work outside of the home, and parents can be secure knowing that their family will take care of them into old age. Quality family services do not depend upon financial resources like they do in the United States, and there is really no extra expense on the part of the government. As a result, there are fewer kids who are "left behind" or who fall through the cracks, contributing to a more egalitarian society, at least as far as children are concerned. Paradoxically, the relative equality children enjoy early in life dissipates later as jobs and promotions go to those with the right family connections rather than to those who deserve it. Just the same, Macedonia offers an example of how a society can produce well-adjusted, healthy children, even in the absence of financial resources. Considering the extent to which income plays a determining factor in so much of a child's well-being in the United States, we would do well to at least take notice.

PART II

On Institutions

CHAPTER 5

The Paradox, and Promise, of Education in the Global Era

Despite presiding over one of the smallest countries in Europe, the government in Macedonia deals with more than its fair share crises. In 2015 alone there was a massive wiretapping scandal that revealed egregious corruption at the very highest levels of government, an international refugee crisis as thousands of migrants were stranded on its border with Greece, and a brief but violent armed insurrection by Albanian militants that left multiple dead on both sides. With so many pressing issues of such national and international significance, one could understand if lower profile domestic matters were tabled for future consideration. Stories about health care, education, and infrastructure do not have nearly the same capacity to capture the interest of lawmakers and politicians when such serious issues come to the fore. And still, among all of those competing priorities, an item that rose to the top of the legislative docket, and subsequently mobilized thousands of protesters for weeks at a time, was educational reform.

One of the top reasons why the government placed something as mundane as educational reform so high on the political agenda speaks to its central role in yet another crisis: the mass exodus of young people. In recent years, universities throughout the Balkans have become notorious for a range of unsavory academic scandals, prompting hundreds of promising students to nurture their academic talents elsewhere. Many of them will become productive members of society in more prosperous countries and never return, further depleting the level of human capital that Macedonia and other Balkan countries so desperately need. Revamping educational policy is an attempt to do something, anything, to improve the credibility of diplomas from the country's universities and keep talented and educated young people at home.

The reforms include rather basic measures aimed at improving academic standards and accountability for both students and educators. At the high school level, the new policies introduce more rigorous standardized testing, ostensibly to raise the bar on admissions to domestic universities. At the university level, professors are now subject to quantifiable performance evaluations, including a requirement to publish a certain number of articles per year in reputable academic journals. On paper, these reforms come across as a necessary but unremarkable step in the right direction. Most American universities have similar performance metrics, and state governments are constantly implementing new testing policies at the high school level. Perhaps more surprising than education reform being taken up as an issue in the midst of so many national crises is the fact that such standards did not exist in the first place.

Nonetheless, news of the changes compelled students to stage a sit-in at the main public university, effectively shutting it down for weeks, and further mass demonstrations temporarily paralyzed the capital. The story was even picked up on the BBC and there was a very active reddit thread devoted to the subject. Opponents charged that the hastily implemented reforms were just another attempt by the government to exert its control over universities, which harbored some of the last remaining pockets of intellectual resistance to an increasingly authoritarian administration. University faculty who criticized the government could more easily be sidelined with bureaucratic procedures, such as failing to meet the performance metrics. Those who voiced support could be advanced by the same means, since the Ministry of Education could simply declare that professors with favorable views were performing well. All the while the new policies would do nothing to address the deeper issues that plague the education system, such as corruption, politicization, and a disturbing lack of ethics.

As anyone who remembers the good old days will tell you, it was not always like this. The education system was a source of pride in Yugoslavia, and doctors and professors were highly respected figures in society. There was even a program to bring in university students from other non-aligned countries, especially from those in Africa. Networks and connections still factored into success in the classroom far more than is the case in American universities, but overall the system was viable enough to serve the national interests. So what happened? How could a system that once attracted foreign students seeking better opportunities now have reached such a depth that it compels many of the country's best and brightest to move abroad?

Working as an English teacher and then as a college professor for three years gave me plenty of time to ponder that question. The simple and obvious answer is that Macedonia can no longer rely on the relative wealth and stability of Yugoslavia, whose government officially opened the country's first university as recently as 1949. The subsequent collapse has been especially hard on Macedonia, which was already the poorest constituent republic, and education is just one of many casualties. In broad terms, that narrative is certainly true, but there are a number of interrelated factors, including moves to privatize and politicize education, the globalization of academics, and even cultural practices that have a combined influence on the state of Macedonia's current education system.

The privatization of universities began shortly after the fall of communism in Eastern Europe. Prior to that universities were state-run institutions that catered almost exclusively to the intellectual elite and to those who were truly interested in academics. Since the communist system depended mostly on industry and basic services, obtaining a university degree was not a necessary precondition for employment. A high school degree was more than sufficient to immediately begin working in any number of trades. Higher skilled jobs still paid higher wages, but lower skilled jobs paid enough to foster a flourishing middle class, as anyone who worked in the 1980s on back will still remind you on a daily basis.

When the system collapsed in the early 1990s, the massive state subsidies that were propping up broad sectors of the economy went with it. Hundreds of factories closed and thousands of jobs disappeared in a matter of months. A new economy based on skills, knowledge, and specialized services took its place, dramatically increasing the demand for higher education. Degrees in tourism management, English language teaching, and especially business management became sought after commodities. Many of the countries in the region, however, had only one state university and were unable to expand fast enough to accommodate so many new students. Dozens of new private universities appeared seemingly overnight, presenting a market-based solution to what appeared to be a simple supply and demand problem. In exchange for thousands of dollars in tuition, students could get easy access to a range of majors that were supposed to help them navigate their way through the transition.

By one measure at least, the move to privatize higher education was successful. Today private universities are highly profitable business ventures that enroll over thirty percent of the university students in the region. In that way they are certainly satisfying the increased demand for higher education. However, they are also notorious for being little more than diploma mills that churn out plagiarized theses and dissertations for a price. Students who are otherwise uninterested in education can easily enroll in obscure majors and be sure that they can exert minimal effort and graduate, as long as they continue paying. The government, for its part, remains hands off because politicians take significant cuts from the profits that these universities bring in. Institutions that resist this sort of meddling are denied accreditation and are forced to close. As the government in my home state of Kentucky once proclaimed, education pays, in this case quite literally.

  The learning outcomes are so poor that some job announcements in Macedonia specify that they will not recognize qualifications from private universities. Undeterred, students continue to pay thousands of dollars to enroll because receiving a diploma, rather than a quality education, is the ultimate goal. The importance of having a diploma in hand speaks to the intense politicization of nearly all aspects of Macedonian society, including the workplace. Since many positions are awarded on the basis of connections rather than qualifications, graduates can be confident that they will secure employment *preku vrski* (through connections) whether they study or not. The system creates a perverse incentive to finish rather than learn. As long as the person filling the position technically meets the educational requirements, the company can follow the letter of the law requiring a certain degree in a specific field. On paper the person is "qualified", and in the Balkans a physical piece of paper with an official stamp on it carries a surprising amount of weight.

Political parties also use private institutions as feeders so that they can provide the illusion that their ministers were appointed based on merit rather than connections. Dozens of high ranking officials in governments throughout the region have glorified academic titles from private universities that were either plagiarized or granted under dubious pretenses. Even the more respected public institutions have not completely escaped the grasp of politics. Some professors have open allegiances with political parties and use the weight of their academic titles to push certain agendas, as referenced in the introductory chapter of this book. The massive student protests were partially a reaction against that sort of politicization at the state university.

Lost in the corruption of the private system and the politicization of higher education in general are the many professors and aspiring students that are intelligent, capable, and hard-working individuals. They do the best they can under difficult circumstances, including low salaries, substandard facilities, and political pressure. Perhaps the greatest difficulty, however, is the struggle to keep pace in the globalized academic environment of the 21st century.

Globalization in academics presents a sort of paradox for the developing world. On the surface it would seem that advances in communication technologies and the digitization of virtually all academic output would be equalizing forces that democratize access to information. Physical books and papers can only travel so fast, plus they cost money to print, ship, and store. In the past, if a university library did not have physical possession of those hard copies, it was as if they did not exist. Digitized information, by contrast, is instantly diffused and stored online at no extra cost to the end user. Theoretically it follows that in the digital age, information no longer faces the geographic and financial barriers that once disadvantaged places on the global periphery. In reality, the benefits have mostly accrued in places that were already centers of knowledge production, creating an even wider disparity than previously existed.

One of the primary causes of that disparity is that access to most high-quality academic journals requires subscription fees that cost hundreds and sometimes thousands of dollars per publication. At most large American universities, student fees cover the cost of those subscriptions, and there are usually partnerships with other university libraries to loan the titles they do not carry. These services enable professors based in high-income countries like the United States to produce some of the most significant academic publications in the world, but they also cost the institutions millions of dollars per year. Not only do professors in Macedonia lack that sort of institutional support, they are paid less than 8,000 dollars a year on average and are unable to cover the cost of subscriptions on their own.

In addition, the globalization of academics has significantly increased the importance of English language. A large proportion of Macedonian professors grew up in Yugoslavia, where the expression "speak Serbian so the whole world will understand you" was taken as conventional wisdom. Back then English was one elective language among many others, including Russian, French, and German. It was nice to know, but certainly not mandatory. Having not been exposed to academic-level English until later in life, many of Macedonia's older professors struggle to meet the exceptionally high drafting skills required to get accepted in scholarly publications. Journal editors often request that articles be proofread and corrected by a native speaker in order to be considered for publication, but these services can cost hundreds of dollars per submission.

As a result, native English speakers and academics from countries with long histories of English language education like Holland and Sweden have tremendous advantages. They are able to use those advantages to produce some of the most widely cited publications in the world, thereby shaping the direction of international academic discourse. This is especially the case in the social sciences, which tend to be on the vanguard of liberal issues such as LGBT rights and racial injustice. Such topics are either untenable to research in far more socially conservative environments like Macedonia or have no cultural reference point, confining academics there to a smaller range of issues that may not find traction with western reviewers and editors.

There are alternatives to journals that allow Macedonian professors to showcase their work and learn about the work of others. Academic conferences, for example, can be a very effective way for scholars to get exposed to new research and to present their own work to a specialized audience. They can also help foster collaborations between people who otherwise may have never met. But registration fees can be rather steep, even by western standards, not to mention the travel expenses involved. Some Macedonian institutions can barely make payroll every month, much less provide travel funding for conferences. To further complicate matters, many of the world's premier conferences are held in countries that require Macedonian passport holders to first obtain a visa, such as the United States, the United Kingdom, Canada, and Australia. Just to apply for a US travel visa costs 160 dollars, which can amount to nearly half of most professors' monthly income, and there is no guarantee an application will even be approved.

To be fair, globalization has opened new doors for academics in Macedonia, especially for those who were educated abroad and have a strong network of contacts at foreign institutions. Drawing upon that international network they can more easily access literature at western universities or co-author a publication with a colleague abroad. They are more likely to have been exposed to academic English and trained in how to prepare journal articles. Salaries are still lower than their counterparts in the West, but they are able to find their way into respected international journals and conferences. For the majority of professors, however, globalization in academics has presented more obstacles than opportunities.

An entire parallel academic universe has emerged to help those with fewer connections and resources overcome those obstacles. Open access journals, for example, charge the authors to publish and allow the consumers to access the content for free. Even though the submission fees can be high, and the articles are not always part of the academic mainstream, this model does provide some access to research literature for those who would otherwise be without. There are also dozens of conferences throughout Eastern Europe that allow anyone who pays to submit a paper with no requirement for actually showing up and presenting. The submissions will then appear in the conference program or book of abstracts, which provides some measure of publicity and potentially grants exposure to other research in the field. Most importantly, it helps professors advance in their careers back home because national ministries of education reward quantity rather than quality when it comes to academic production.

Cast in a positive light, one could argue that these models remove the financial and linguistic obstacles that now characterize higher education in the age of globalization. But they also introduce monetary incentives for publishers and conferences to accept virtually any manuscript as long as the author pays the submission fees. In the face of pressure to compete with academics who have far more resources, the willingness to engage in such practices is understandable, even if they lower the overall quality of scientific output and weaken the reputation of the professors.

Cultural practices comprise a final set of factors that influence the quality of the higher education system in Macedonia. Unfortunately, they are also the most difficult to change because they are so firmly entrenched. One such cultural practice is the rigid social hierarchy that characterizes Balkan society. Those who are at the top of the hierarchy are expected to openly display their authority over lower groups, whether the power relations are between a boss and employees or a professor and students. As such, professors generally do not tolerate dissenting viewpoints from students, even if the resulting discussion can be made into a teachable moment. They may even take personal offense at being questioned. Students comply with the hierarchy, even if they are not necessarily in agreement, because of the fear that stepping out of line will bring retribution in the form of lower grades.

Power structures govern the relations between professors and students to greater or lesser extents throughout the world, but educational outcomes are actually better in places where there is less distance between professors and students. This can be hard to accept in a society that places so much value on strong, decisive, and hierarchical leadership, as was made obvious to me when a professor from Finland came to the school where I was working to recruit students. During his recruitment pitch he explained that in proudly egalitarian Scandinavia professors take pride in being on the same social level with their students and even encourage them to be on a first name basis. Doing so, he explained, has helped Finland climb to the top of worldwide academic rankings and was an important draw for talented international students. In the audience the students snickered in disbelief while the professors squirmed in discomfort at the thought of such a radical breach of social protocol. Under his breath one colleague turned to me and said "It's not like that here" through gritted teeth, as if to reassure himself that he was, in fact, correct.

In order to reinforce the social hierarchy in the classroom, professors and teachers employ old-fashioned teaching methods that stress memorization and precision rather than creativity or problem solving. Doing so allows them to maintain control by removing the need to debate the information being presented, but it also goes against the recommendations of numerous pedagogical experts that encourage devoting significant class time to group work and activities. As a consequence, students in Macedonia have become accustomed to learning by heart, leaving them ill-prepared for employment in a modern economy that requires creativity, independent thinking, and problem solving skills. Of more immediate concern, however, is that this method of instruction is very conducive to cheating. Exam grades are largely based on the extent to which students are able to accurately reproduce the material they were given. Knowing this, students prepare lists and even short answers ahead of time and simply copy them onto the exam. Professors are mostly content to look the other way, especially if the student has political connections or important parents.

Pedagogical style aside, there are other cultural aspects of the widespread cheating phenomenon that plagues the education system. In the Balkans, and indeed in many other parts of the non-Western world, people just have a different viewpoint on the ethics of cheating, or on what constitutes dishonesty more generally. The way different cultures play and appreciate soccer is perhaps the easiest way to illustrate that point. Anyone who has seen a soccer game has witnessed a player dive to draw a penalty, embellish a common foul to elicit a yellow card, or fake an injury to waste time. For some, those are dishonest acts of poor sportsmanship that are tantamount to cheating. For others, they are intelligent strategies that can help a team win, which is, after all, the whole point. In the former perspective, the rules are black and white, so following both the letter and the spirit of the law is the only way to behave ethically. Failure to do so merits an appropriate punishment. In the latter perspective, the lines defining the rules are blurry, and the ethics of even following those rules in the first place depend upon the situation. If someone does not exactly follow the spirit of the law but still gets a positive result without getting caught, such as a passing exam grade, then there is no reason for anyone to be upset.

The Balkan viewpoint on academic conduct is definitely more akin to the latter perspective. I learned this lesson early on while teaching English to a group of high school students. We would often begin class with a short game of trivia as a warmup activity, just to get them thinking and speaking in English. My intent was to ask them basic questions, like what is the largest city in Europe, give them time to think about it, and then answer in a complete sentence. Whether they got the question right or wrong was irrelevant because they would still be practicing

English either way, and we could build a discussion around their answers.

I got the idea from my days as a graduate student playing bar trivia back in the United States. This being the 21st century, the most important rule was to not use phones to look up any answer. With very few exceptions, at least at the places I played, almost no one ever did. Trying to play trivia in my Macedonian classroom was a different story all together. It was, in the parlance of the locals, *katastrofa*. No matter how much I emphasized that there were no prizes for the winners, or that we were just doing a warmup activity, or that the game was in no way linked to their grades, students still devised ways to look up the answers on their phones, without fail, every time. Running the risk of getting the "wrong" answer just did not make sense to them when they could easily get the "right" answer on their phones, even if it that was not the point of the game.

Although the stakes in the preceding anecdote were rather low, these different views regarding proper academic conduct scale all the way up the administrative hierarchy. In one such instance I witnessed a high-ranking professor question a student's intelligence because he did not produce a fake medical document so that he could be excused from an exam. "This was stupid," the professor told him dismissively, pointing to her head for emphasis. "You should have just turned in a fake excuse like everyone else and we would have accepted it," and she looked over at me awaiting an affirming nod of the head. Strictly speaking, she was correct. On paper the policy stated that students needed a medical excuse to reschedule an exam. Whether or not the excuse was legitimate or even from a doctor was not immediately relevant. For the young man, it was a valuable lesson for the future: following the rules is like playing a game, and you should always use whatever tools you have to try and win.

On another occasion a colleague who had completed a portion of his graduate studies in the United States informed me that our higher education system relied too heavily on trust. He explained that in lieu of a traditional final exam, his American professor had given the class ten questions that they could prepare at home. Indeed, in social sciences disciplines, especially at the graduate level, that is probably the most common way to administer an exam. When they felt they were ready, they could turn in their answers any time during finals week.

"None of the students even *offered* to collaborate!" he explained in wide eyed disbelief, "and the professors didn't even bother to check if we had shared answers!"

From his perspective, the students had wasted a good opportunity for everyone to benefit, and the professors were at best shockingly naïve to think that they would just work in an honest manner. It seemed obvious to him that the best student should just copy the relevant passages from the book verbatim.

That way all of the questions would have precise answers, and they could be easily copied for the rest of the class to turn in as well. Not only that, future generations of students would have the exact questions and answers. The professor would be forced to give perfect scores to everyone because all of the answers would be correct, making the exam invalid. That the purpose of a take-home final in graduate school could be to examine research, drafting, and argumentation skills, and not necessarily to produce one correct answer copied from the book, was completely lost on him.

My colleague's reaction to his experience in American graduate school also illustrates how collectivist social pressures can surface in the sphere of education. In a collectivist culture, such as that of Macedonia and the Balkans in general, friendships are incredibly close, something approaching codependence. If your friend calls, you are expected to answer the phone. If someone wants to go out for coffee, you are expected to say yes, even if you are studying or otherwise busy. If you are a good student or show some competence in a subject at school, you are expected to share your work with the group so that everyone can benefit.

To an outsider from an individualist culture, such as that of the United States, those expectations may seem trivial or easy to dismiss. People get busy, or tired, or have other obligations, and they certainly cannot be expected to complete someone else's work. That is because individualist cultures base success more on accomplishments than relationships. There are measurable benefits and intrinsic satisfaction to completing a project as an individual, whether in school or in the workplace. Likewise, there are built-in social and professional repercussions associated with appropriating the work of others. At best, copying from someone else would be seen as lazy and unprofessional, and at worst it would be considered a punishable act of academic misconduct.

In collectivist societies there is a different cost-benefit calculus at play. Since nearly all aspects of social and professional advancement are based on connections, failure to comply with the expected social norms can have real consequences down the line. Not allowing a friend to copy, for example, especially if you are the more capable student, could damage the close relationships upon which you depend for any number of social benefits. These problems are magnified to an even greater extent in small countries like Macedonia, where the size of the population and lack of opportunities significantly limit one's ability to circumvent the need for connections.

To be sure, educational policy is something that is fiercely debated in the halls of government throughout the world. Macedonia is by no means unique in that regard, especially among its fellow peripheral countries. All of them are trying to adjust to the modern era of unfettered openness and competition, and there are no easy answers. At a minimum, private institutions need far more regulation, more public investment is needed to help professors keep pace with the academic mainstream, and both of those reforms must be free of politics. Those are tall, but not impossible, orders to fill. Cultural practices in education generally take much longer to change, but through greater dialogue and productive engagement with international partners, they too can be adapted over time. These difficulties notwithstanding, serious educational reform is in Macedonia's national interest, far more so than the monuments and urban renewal projects on which the government has chosen to spend public money.

CHAPTER 6

Yugonostalgia and Capitalism in Europe's Wild, Wild East

As a kid from the 80s with an oddly strong interest in geography, I was among those people who had at least heard of Yugoslavia. I remember looking at it on a map and noting that Belgrade was its capital, and I remember its red, white, and blue flag with that red star in the middle outlined in gold (I was, uh, kind of a dork, but it really did prepare me for future domination in trivia, so that's a positive). From my perspective, even as a child, it was a large Eastern European country that was stuck in the grips of communism, where Levis jeans sold for two hundred dollars and the national car was the Yugo. Given the chance, I assumed, people would find a way to escape the dark shadows of communism and into the warm, loving embrace of capitalism and democracy somewhere in the West. I imagined this gray, soulless existence consisting of housing projects and behemoth factories, much the way I picture North Korea in the present day.

Little did I know that at the same time I was forming my impression of Yugoslavia, the man who was to be my future father-in-law was pondering a move to the United States. He had received a work permit to be a full-time mechanic in New York, where some of his acquaintances already lived. They were to help him get settled and learn the language, and once he got on his feet he could send for his wife and two daughters. Plus, there was an established Balkan expat community in New York that would help make the transition easier for all of them. The year was about 1986, and instead of jumping at the opportunity to dash off to the land of the free, he took a look at the offer, considered his life back in Yugoslavia, and said, "No thanks, I'm good here." He had the chance to escape to the other side and live out the American Dream, and he declined.

As it turns out, life in Yugoslavia was not at all like I (and many others in the United States) had imagined it to be. It is true that it was run as a semi-authoritarian communist country, but it allowed far more social and economic freedoms than did the USSR and its satellite states, and certainly more than neighboring Albania. In fact, Yugoslavia was one of the few countries in Europe to actively oppose the hegemony of the USSR-USA dichotomy and did things more or less on its own terms. Unlike many countries during the Cold War, Yugoslav passport holders enjoyed unrestricted visa-free travel between East and West. In 1984, the country was also credited with giving the outside world a positive image of socialism when it became the first communist state to host the Winter Olympics in Sarajevo. The Games were viewed then, as they still are now, as a tremendous success. The economy was "something in between" socialism and market-based capitalism, and a large proportion of the population had a dignified existence that included a yearly vacation and discretionary spending money.

There were limits to civil liberties, especially as Americans understand them, and chronic unemployment pushed hundreds of thousands of its citizens to find work abroad. It was certainly not a utopia were everyone was perfectly content, but life was mostly good, especially from Macedonia's perspective. Along with Kosovo, it was the least developed region of the country and therefore received a massive influx of federal funds, much to the chagrin of Slovenia and some of the other wealthier regions. Yugoslavia established Macedonia's first universities, enabled it to develop an industrial base, and invested heavily in its infrastructure. When Skopje was levelled by an earthquake in 1963, the federal government used its resources to rebuild the city, and many of those projects are still in use today.

Even though Yugoslavia fell apart when the communist system collapsed 25 years ago, Yugonostalgia still weighs heavy on the minds of almost everyone in Macedonia who remembers it. During the three years that I lived there hardly a day went by when someone did not mention Yugoslavia, socialism, Tito, or that things used to be better. Usually they were all discussed at the same time in one long, wistful trip down memory lane. Even some people born *after* the breakup can get Yugonostalgic when they start to reflect upon the present state of their country. It is not an exaggeration to say that almost any time I met someone over the age of 40, the conversation would go something like this:

"How long have you been here? You learned Macedonian pretty well."

"What state are you from? Is that near New Jersey?"

"How do you like it here? Yeah, life is good here if you have money."

"Did you know that we were part of Yugoslavia and that it was way better than now? Let me tell you about it as if you are hearing it for the first time, again."

Seriously, that is a pretty accurate portrayal of a standard introductory conversation.

It was also explained to me how socialism worked, how much people liked it, and how smart Tito was (who had been dead for over 35 years at that point, by the way). For good measure, they would then throw in how much better life is in Macedonia than in the West, even if that person had never been to the West and had no means of comparison. Then I would be told about how students from Libya used to come study in Yugoslavia and that Gaddafi was one of the best world leaders, along with Tito of course, because of all the things he had done for his people. Talk of the good old days would not be complete without the assertion that the United States broke up Yugoslavia out of jealousy and is therefore largely to blame for the current malaise. That last point I find interesting because the United

States is also accused of being completely ignorant on all things politics and history, including Yugoslavia, so it is not clear to me how it could simultaneously be jealous and ignorant. Not to mention that ethnic tensions started simmering shortly after Tito's death, a full 11 years before the collapse, and that economic difficulties worsened throughout the socialist economies of Eastern Europe during the 1980s, but I digress.

The persistence of Yugonostalgia is all the more impressive when one considers that Macedonia was officially a socialist federal republic under Yugoslavia for a mere 45 years. To state it another way, there are many people alive today who were born before its existence, and an entire generation has come of age in the 25 years following its demise. But that short amount of time was sufficient to leave an indelible mark on the collective memory of the country and to significantly affect its transition to capitalism and democracy. Before going to Macedonia I attributed Yugonostalgia and the slow pace of development to "the legacy of the communist past," and assumed I knew what that phrase meant. But if someone had asked me to explain what, exactly, that legacy entailed, I could only rely on vague generalities gleaned from people who had yet to grow weary from their Cold War victory laps. Essentially, the legacy of communism was, you know, bad. That's not to say that the legacy does not exist, because it certainly does, but it has many layers, some of which I knew existed, and some of which are more nuanced and are difficult to unravel from deep-rooted cultural tendencies.

The parts of the complex legacy of communism of which I was already aware were mostly things I had learned from the media. For example, television and movies often portray Eastern European customer service as, well, lacking in service. I still remember seeing a news story about the opening of the first McDonald's in Moscow shortly after the fall of the USSR and watching the manager trying to convince his workers to smile, SMILE! SMILE! Customer service, at least as Americans understand it, was just not a necessary skill during the communist time. Bureaucracy was everything, and customer service was just another form of bureaucracy. People with connections got good service, just like in a bureaucracy, and everybody else had to wait and be annoyed. Plus, smiling at strangers for no reason is a sign of a crazy person in Eastern Europe, not a friendly gesture intended to make someone feel welcome. Smiles do not make the bureaucracy run smoother, that's what connections are for.

Although times have changed somewhat, in part because so many young people have worked in customer service jobs abroad and have brought back new habits and expectations, that practice is still pretty widespread in Macedonia. At the market the teller is likely to ignore you while she aggressively scans and throws your items to the side, which you will then bag yourself.

At the currency exchange desk, the clerk will likely toss your money back at you while barely acknowledging your existence. If you purchased a faulty or unwanted item and then try to return it the store will act like it was your mistake for buying such a low-quality item in the first place, even though that implies they sell junk. Waiters can be abrupt and inattentive, even annoyed that you are interrupting them from their conversation with their colleagues, although restaurant service in Skopje can be pretty good at places tourists are more likely to visit. The primary difference is that they are not going to come by and ask you if you need anything, so you will have to call them over if you want anything, which can feel awkward for an American where that is considered rude.

    Macedonian customer service is so poor that readjusting to the United States after living over there for a while can be shocking at first. I had kind of gotten used to the struggle and drudgery of needing to have "my guy" to get anything done, which is why a routine interaction at the DC airport sticks with me to this day. When my wife and I came back to the United States on a summer visit, she went to the foreign passport control line, and I went to the much shorter citizen line. I asked one of the workers if she might come in the line with me since we were married and traveling together and the lady immediately opened the rope saying, "Of course, you're family! She doesn't have to wait over there!" She smiled and continued to make polite conversation before telling us to have a good day. We felt like VIPs, even though the lady was just doing her job and it was really nothing out of the ordinary.

On the way back to Skopje, we had the reverse situation with the passport lines at the Alexander the Great Airport. She waited in the citizen line, and I waited in the much longer, much slower international line. When she asked if I could come to the line with her, the worker shot back with a rhetorical question, "Is he a citizen? Then no!" And that was it. I waited in what passes for a line, which is more like a mass with no shape, and she waited on the other side of the security for an extra half hour. When I greeted the officer at the passport control station in Macedonian, which I thought was a nice gesture, he ignored me, stamped the passport, and tossed it back at me instead of handing it to me. And this is in a country that really needs tourists and foreign residents. In hindsight, I realize that we were making a rookie mistake and that I should have just gone in the line anyway and acted like I own the place. In future instances, that is exactly what I did and it worked like a charm.

Nowhere is evidence of the old times more obvious than in the public sector, where aggressively sour dispositions prevail and connections are essentially the only way things get done. Examples of this are endless, but one particularly frustrating experience stands out in my memory. When my wife decided to apply to graduate school in the United States, she needed official transcripts from St. Cyril and Methodius University, which is Macedonia's primary state university. As of 2015 there was still no system to order copies online, so we went in person to the Office of Student Affairs, which works between 11 and 2 only. We got there at 11:15 to find a lady intensely playing solitaire in an otherwise empty office. Intense solitaire, it turns out, is a staple of the Macedonian bureaucratic workplace. We asked for two envelopes with a school seal so that we could send official transcripts to foreign institutions, and she stopped her game, exhaled loudly, and said, "Child! Do you realize I'm working in Student Affairs? I don't give envelops!" Oh, side note, calling grown people "boy" or "girl" or "child" is not considered rude in Macedonia, although it is still difficult to see how that can be interpreted any other way. Yet again, I digress.

    We were told to go to another room where they could help us, except that door was locked and the people inside did not feel interrupting their conversation to open up. So we had to go up two flights of stairs to find the Dean's secretary, who told us to go back to that locked door because those are the people who were supposed to help us. We asked her to call and say that she sent us, that way they would be more likely to open the door because it would look like we had "our person" working with us. Back down two flights of stairs we knocked on the same door, entered, requested the envelops, and got out of there in about 15 seconds. The system works! It just takes about a half hour to accomplish something that should take ten seconds, not to mention lots of frustration and, of course, connections.

Those sorts of experiences are exactly how I expected the legacy of communism to play out. Back in the day there was only one political party headed by a single leader with far-reaching control over most aspects of civil society. If you wanted to get anything official done, you had to work your way through the party hierarchy until someone high enough took an interest. People got used to that, and that bureaucratic legacy has persisted to this day. That part is straightforward enough. It was only through living there and talking to people that the less obvious aspects of the legacy of communism became apparent.

One of those aspects is the way that the average adult understands how the economy functions. Despite the painful economic changes endured during the transition to capitalism, ask anyone over 40 how to bring back the relative prosperity they remember from before and they will reflexively say that the government should invest in more factories. So entrenched are those memories of the good old days that the politicians often appeal to public nostalgia by proudly citing how many new factories were opened under their administrations, knowing that there is a certain amount of political capital to be gained. People need jobs, factories employ a lot of people, so we need more factories. In the past government created those factories, fed them contracts, and guaranteed them a market. It all seems so simple, and it can be hard for older citizens to understand why that can't just happen again.

In the United States, a flourishing small business sector is more commonly seen as the catalyst for economic development rather than government investment in factories. The government does, of course, invest in factories in the United States, but this is not how most people *imagine* that the economy functions. We praise small businesspeople who "pull themselves up by their bootstraps" and create something new. Entrepreneurs like Steve Jobs, Bill Gates, and Elon Musk are as close as it gets to a non-athlete hero in American culture. Although Macedonia does have successful entrepreneurs, the culture of entrepreneurship is still struggling to catch on for a variety of reasons. First, a lack of credit and capital present serious obstacles to acting on most business ideas. Plus, almost all material goods have to be shipped in from the outside without the benefit of a common economic area such as the European Union. But the biggest obstacle of all is dealing with the government's legion of economic henchmen, who run the country's business sector like a mafia enterprise.

Successful businesses have a way of getting inspected excessively if they do not play nice, and bureaucracy can be rather tedious and expensive for those who try to circumvent the system. In fact, the primary reason there are no McDonald's in Macedonia is not because the population is making a statement about healthy living, but because the owner of the franchise refused to share the profits with certain members of the government, who in turn revoked his right to own the franchise. Because of maneuvers like these, a very small number of people in the government's inner circle have gotten seriously rich, while those on the outside are often discouraged from ever pursuing their own ventures in the first place. Not exactly the sort of business environment capable of fostering innovation and inspiring creative new ideas.

The communist legacy also instilled a different mentality when it comes to work, which is surprisingly persistent and has the ability to cross generational divides. Some of my students who went to the United States on a work-and-travel program, for example, were disillusioned by how much they were expected to work while at, you know, work, and they were all born years after the fall of socialism. Lots of young people who migrate abroad likewise report back that life in the West is too stressful because working conditions are too strenuous. They are not necessarily used to staying on task for hours at a time, having such rigid breaks, and occasionally having to work more during peak times in the case of a restaurant. Even if they did not live through it, they are drawing upon attitudes concerning the workplace and professionalism that have stuck around since the old days of Yugoslavia.

Back then, work started at 7:30 and ended at 3:30, Monday to Friday. There were long coffee breaks, cigarette breaks, and extended lunches, not to mention the guaranteed four-week paid vacation. If things were not exactly as they should be, it was fine, someone would fix it. Anyone who has driven a Yugo can probably surmise that it did not matter all that much to the workers at the factory if the car was well-built. They were cheap, they drove like a car is supposed to most of the time, and when they didn't, there were plenty of mechanics who needed the business and could fix them cheaply. Good enough. It did not matter if you did not put in maximum effort at work because your survival was not tied to the profit margins of a private firm. Companies had liberal expense accounts that included occasional dinners for the employees at a kafana, and they would get New Year's presents for the kids of the workers. It was not unusual at some work places to drink hard liquor at 10 in the morning... on the clock.

    The old system is long gone, but many of those behaviors have proven hard to overcome, including drinking on the job at some workplaces. The most obvious example is the way people start the work day. At a typical Macedonian office, the first thing most people do when they get to work is make coffee or tea and then sit and chat with their colleagues for about 30 to 45 minutes. Most American workplaces would view that behavior as an unproductive waste of company time and expect you to either drink coffee before work or at your desk while you are working. My colleagues were perpetually interested in the to-go coffee mug that I brought from home. "You're so American!" they would say, "You drink coffee in your car just like in the movies!" Needless to say, the idea of a drive-thru coffee place is kind of a nonstarter over there. It seems like a soulless manipulation of the beloved institution of sitting for an extended amount of time over coffee and "enjoying," as they would say.

  When they are back at work, most people seem content to just finish their basic tasks and to relax, or again, to enjoy. If it was not something they were specifically assigned, they are not likely to spend their time doing more work. Maybe they will take a cigarette break, go sit with their colleagues once more, and probably have another coffee or tea. They will almost certainly make multiple personal phone calls and have long, detailed, and relatively loud conversations. This is quite different from what I was used to in the American workplace, where it was understood that once you finish the assigned tasks you should then find new ones on your own without being told, and you should definitely not spend much time on personal calls while on the clock. These differences stem from an understanding of professionalism that does not necessarily value productivity and efficiency. Relationships, both at work and at home, are more important, as evidenced by the centrality of coffee time and the need to be on the phone so much.

There are other factors that influence how the people of Macedonia interact with capitalism that can be difficult to untangle from the clean, convenient package that we call the "communist legacy." Some of those factors are cultural, and some of them are reactions to the present economic circumstances. Among those in their late 50s and early 60s, for example, it is exceedingly common to hear them count down the months and years to when they can finally retire and start living on their social security check. If you are there, pay attention and you will probably notice that basically everyone knows the exact day when they will retire, even if that day is many years in the future. People talk very openly about exactly how much their monthly check will be and what they are planning on doing with the money. Even among the younger generation there are those who want to live in a wealthier country not because the salaries are higher but because the government benefits for the poor are more generous. Almost everyone in Macedonia knows of someone who has moved to Western Europe, gets on all of the government programs, and has no intention of working. Although that is not a fair characterization of the diaspora in general, because there many others from Macedonia who make important professional contributions to countries around the world, it is a tendency that is worth at least acknowledging.

There is a segment of the American population that would paint this eagerness to receive public assistance as an example of government dependency that was learned during the communist time. There may be some truth to that, but it is also true that there is some form of financial logic underpinning these tendencies. Most people will actually receive a bigger check in retirement or on public assistance than they will making an honest wage because the benefits of capitalism that were supposed to accrue have been so minimal in Macedonia. The natural retort is that new economic systems take time to implement and cultural shifts take even more time, and that it took the United States over a century to figure out how to harness the economic potential of capitalism. All true statements (if not also reductionist), but that's an easy position to take from the outside. As the transition approaches its third decade, generations of people live their lives and would like to have a piece of the pie. At the moment most people do not have a legitimate shot at even the opportunity to *earn* a piece, must less have it handed to them.

Macedonians (and Balkan people in general) also have a particular way of viewing money that again could be product of the institutional legacy of communism, but could just as easily be a cultural difference. There is a strong tendency towards passive acceptance of life's circumstances, not unlike the fatalistic outlook on life that characterizes the Appalachian culture where I am from. Many people are content with living for today, or to be even more precise, living for the moment. Even though salaries are low and sometimes intermittent, there is no shortage of people who make decisions out of temporary convenience that further impoverish them.

The easiest example that comes to mind is the habit of parking in illegal spots, including on the sidewalk or just right on the road, because it is a little closer, but then getting a parking ticket or having to pay the towing fee. People will tell you that they have to park like that because there is no other parking, but what they mean is that there is no other *free* parking nearby and that they would rather risk paying over fifty dollars to park closer than paying one dollar to park correctly and then walk a little. In case it was not clear by now, fifty dollars can buy a lot of things in Macedonia and should, for most people, be something to think twice about before spending. Betting parlors are always busy, and kafanas are full of people who just got paid and want to go out and have a good time, even if that means that they will be short on money for at least the rest of the month, and possibly longer. The attitude seems to be, "I have money now, tomorrow will work itself out." There is also a tendency to constantly gripe about having no money, but then to go on vacation to the beach in Greece and or to stay out until the wee hours of the morning. Remember *Makedonska rabota* from the second chapter? Because now would be an appropriate time to shrug, sigh, and "Makedonska rabota" in a resigned manner.

For someone coming from the United States, living in the moment can be a refreshing change of pace. In the academic career track that I was on prior to moving there was constant pressure to be looking at what's next on the horizon. How can I put in my time now to get a better position at this higher profile university? What should I be doing to put myself in line for promotion in six years? What project should I be doing next so I can raise my professional profile? Can this person I just met help me advance my career in any way?

This is, of course, how most professions function in the United States, and there are material rewards for being ambitious and career-driven in that way. There are also social costs, primarily in the form of weaker relationships that result from the need to constantly move in pursuit of the next best thing. It can be freeing to just be content with what you have and where you are at that time and place, although I have seen expats get overly romantic about this notion. People in Macedonia live in the moment, in part anyway, because the lack of stability sort of forces them to do so. Plans are difficult to realize because the only avenue in which ambitious people can reasonably advance is politics. Salaries come and go, jobs can evaporate for no good reason, contracts are less than ironclad, and the government can intervene in strange and unpredictable ways. Under those circumstances, people learn to enjoy the moment and live with what they have, because there is a real possibility that they might not have it tomorrow.

This attitude is especially evident in the older generation, many of whom have a legitimately difficult time understanding why so many young people would want to leave Macedonia. From their perspective, a young person who lives rent-free in a portion of their parents' house, makes a few hundred euros a month, and has a car that runs reasonably well is all set. If they have new tiles in the kitchen, walls with a fresh coat of paint, and new windows that don't cause a draft, which we all know is the source of many ailments, then the question becomes: What else could they possibly want? Why would they want to go slave away in the West when they could just stay put and have their basic needs met? In the past, that was enough, even living the dream. There was no desire for much more because there was no possibility for much more.

Suffice it to say that at least for a segment of the younger generation, living the dream has taken on a different meaning. Many of them not only want better pay so they can afford more material goods, they also want better working conditions than the country currently offers. The term "working conditions" conjures up images of dark and dank sweatshop factories that offer very low pay and long hours. Such establishments do exist in Macedonia, but I use the term here to refer to what the workplace experience is like for the average person, regardless of where they work. Working conditions become an especially important factor after a person is exposed to a different way of doing things in the West, which is the case for a large proportion of young people. Although I have had many similar conversations since, one interaction I had with a young guy seeking advice about moving to the United States from Macedonia illustrates this point well.

The year before he had gone on a work-and-travel program and was planning on returning to the United States in the summer, except this time he was going to overstay his visa and live there indefinitely. He explained that he had worked at a Pizza Hut and had what he called a "burning desire" to get back. Nothing against Pizza Hut, but I never knew that a minimum wage job in the lower end of the service industry could inspire such a reaction, so I pressed him on the matter. Living as an undocumented immigrant brings with it many difficulties, I explained, and the money that he would make at Pizza Hut and similar jobs would not go as far as he expected after he settled into life there. What I really wanted to know is why he would put himself in that position and risk a lengthy absence from his family for a job at a Pizza Hut.

The answer, it turned out, centered not so much on how much money he would be making, but on his perception of the relationship between bosses and their employees. He explained to me how one time he had gotten an order wrong and a customer angrily approached him, asking him to speak with the manager. Rather than yelling at him and punishing him on the spot, the manager calmly stepped in and dealt with the customer, and then took him aside to instruct him on how to deal with a situation like that in the future. There was no belittling in front of the others, and no reduction in his salary out of punishment. For the rest of the time he worked there he felt protected, secure, and intensely loyal both to the boss and to the company.

As he recounted this experience it was clear how deeply this interaction had moved him, and at the time I could not understand why. His description sounded more like an average day at work in the service industry to me and less like a compelling reason to stay in the United States as an undocumented immigrant. I thought this young man was just like so many other people I have met here who have the mistaken impression that life is easy in wealthy countries. Many people fail to account for the cost of living and the lack of social support when they are adding up their expected earnings and end up disappointed. But after working in Macedonia for a few years, I can completely see where he and so many others are coming from.

At the average workplace in Macedonia, that type of friendly and productive interaction he described with his boss is exceedingly rare, especially in lower ranking positions. The hierarchical nature of the society is reinforced in the workplace, where bosses and other authority figures see themselves as naturally superior. Part of being a "good" boss is creating this persona that is dismissive, demeaning, and unapproachable. While American bosses may pride themselves on having an open-door policy, the boss's door in Macedonia is almost always closed. You knock and enter without being called like a scared mouse. Invariably, the doors are old and hard to open, so you immediately feel like you are on someone else's terms just by struggling to open the door. The boss may or may not even acknowledge you, and once he or she does (but almost always he), he may or may not feel like helping you. The most important thing is that he makes sure you know that he is in a position of authority, and that you need him to accomplish something basic.

    Being the boss and showing authority, however arbitrary, is much more important than showing competence, kindness, or even knowledge. It is also a big reason why there is a great aversion to doing jobs that are "beneath" people, such as working as a waitress or in a market. What reasonable person would actively choose to be at the bottom of the hierarchy? The pay is well below what could be considered a living wage, and you have to deal with the whims of a power hungry boss. Of course, people do those jobs, someone has to. It's just that the stigma associated with those jobs is noticeable, and many people actively shun them in the hopes of landing a position with more social prestige through whatever connections they can pull. They want to be the boss, and once they are, they want you to know it.

Most bosses see it within their right to flex their muscles just to show that they can. In the best case scenario, bosses will take a percentage of someone's salary to "punish" them for anything that they deem subpar, however trivial, which can be significant when you're living day-to-day. This sows fear among the workers and re-emphasizes the power structure, as does planting rumors that the salaries will be a few weeks or even months late. When the salaries do finally show up, people have had some time to consider what life would be like if they did not have that income, and they are grateful that they at least got paid. Payday can feel like a holiday as relieved workers start spreading the joyous new with shouts of *"Ima plata! Ima plata!"* (We got paid!). Complaining about any kind of grievance is met with a reminder that nearly all workers are completely replaceable. Indeed, with unemployment so chronically high there are plenty of people who would gladly take their place at a moment's notice, and some bosses seem more than willing to trade experience and institutional knowledge for docility. With so few options, many people are forced to accept these as normal working conditions in Macedonia. But once they are exposed to another way of doing things and are given the opportunity to work in a better environment, they seize it and don't think twice.

As was the case with the education system, Macedonia's struggles with modern capitalism are the result of many factors. Some of them are institutional, such as the legacy of communism that stubbornly continues to wield its influence, and some of them are cultural. Prevailing views on hierarchy, authority, and money management, to name a few cultural differences, can be incongruous with Western-style capitalism. In either case, what is clear in the minds of the citizens is that the lofty promises of the new system have failed to deliver. The implementation of western institutions was supposed to solve national ailments, as anyone who remembers the rhetoric from the early 1990s can attest. They were told that they had been freed from the chains of communism and authoritarianism that were keeping them from reaching their full potential, and that the opportunities were going to be endless. The reality has been another story entirely.

The law and order that was supposed to accompany the new system has been spotty, and the path to success is still through political party membership. The economy depends on lax regulations and low-wage labor that is constantly vulnerable to even lower wage competition elsewhere. All of the drawbacks of the old system such as the bureaucracy, the lack of democracy, state control of the media, and clientelist politics are still around. Missing are the regular paychecks, the affordable housing, and the power of a larger state that has some measure of political relevance. The average person can see that the old system sits crudely on top of the new system, but also that the benefits accrue to a smaller number of people and exclude most everyone else. What's to like?

Rising poverty and unemployment, coupled with the loss of so many sons and daughters that have moved abroad, have increased Yugonostalgia in Macedonia. People need some way, any way, to remind themselves that things were not always like they are now, even if that means being nostalgic for economic conditions that no longer exist anywhere and selectively sugarcoating the past. This sort of nostalgia is akin to the tendency in the United States to uphold the 1950s as an exemplary era to which we should currently return, while ignoring that the global economy has moved on and that severe racial injustices characterized vast swaths of society at that time. In Macedonia there is a tendency to recall the stability and prosperity of Yugoslavia but to ignore the repression of religion, media, and other civil rights. In part, overcoming that repression has set the stage for the emergence of a new radicalism among a segment of the population in Macedonia, Kosovo, Bosnia, and Serbia.

CHAPTER 7
Politics is Everything, and Everything is Politics

Back in my old Kentucky home, we have an expression: It is not polite to talk religion or politics at the dinner table. That maxim would be kind of a problem in Macedonia, because without politics, I'm honestly not sure what people would talk about. At the dinner table, at the *kafana*, in the line at the grocery, over coffee, or anywhere people congregate and talk, politics is everything, and everything is politics. The country's small size makes it almost impossible to ever be far from politics, and many young people are coerced into joining a political party as a condition of keeping their job. They quickly learn that having the right connections with a political party, rather than hard work and personal effort, is the surest way to progress in their careers. That realization kills the ambition of more than a few people who are not willing to play the game, but leaves them with very few options if they choose to stay on the outside of the system. In large countries with big, diverse economies it is possible to move to a different city and avoid local politics. In Macedonia, Skopje is so dominant that leaving the city in search of better opportunities is infeasible, if not impossible in most cases. And so, politics is always there, lurking in the background, just waiting for an opportunity to enter into the conversation.

Even discussing sports, an American staple of mindless

small talk, quickly becomes a political discussion in Macedonia. Here's a brief synopsis of how that plays out. Political parties use their influence to secure sponsorships for their teams, influence player transfers, pressure referees, build new arenas, and even freeze the assets of their sporting/political rivals. Those same party bosses also have extensive connections in the business sector, and they use their companies to finance their teams, even if they technically do not own either one. Fan groups coordinate with party bosses to promote certain agendas, boycott events, and disrupt rival gatherings. Albanians and Macedonians split their allegiances along political party lines, but will band together in ethnic solidarity against the other ethnic group if they need to. And that just scratches the surface of how politics links to something as inconsequential as *sports*, let alone the politicization of religion, employment, media, and pretty much every other institution in the country, public or private. Like the chapter title states, politics is everything, and everything is politics.

But before getting too deep into this topic, a basic overview of the Macedonian political universe is in order. The country has a parliamentary system, and the prime minister is the titular head of state. There is also a certain measure of domestic power invested in the president, similar to the political systems that exist in Russia and Turkey. Although multiple political parties representing a broad range of issues and ethnic groups hold seats in parliament, two rival ethnic Macedonian parties dominate the government, and both of those parties are in coalition with two rival ethnic Albanian parties. Similar to the United States, the two main parties represent the political right and left, but what that division entails in Macedonia is quite different.

To begin with, there is no anguish on either side about the proper role of the state in promoting social welfare like there is in the United States. If anything, the primary impediment to extending social benefits like paid maternity leave and universal healthcare even further is funding, not political opposition from either side. Nearly everyone with a full-time job gets four weeks paid vacation, the elderly depend in large part on the state-run pension system, and most people accept that the government plays an important role in the economy. In that regard, Macedonia is in step with other social democracies in Europe, regardless of the party in power at the moment. Since social welfare is viewed as a basic function of the government, its existence is not a matter of political principle like it is in the United States.

There are also no political debates over the existence of climate change, whether or not to allow regular citizens to purchase assault weapons, or the value of teaching creationism in public schools. The answers are "of course it does," "of course they should not," and "oh you can't be serious." These matters have been resolved both politically and socially, and no further debate is necessary. As discussed in the second chapter, however, there are some rather regressive elements to the society that are reflected in the electorate, such as the pervasive view that homosexuality is a mental illness. Needless to say, LGBT rights barely register on the Macedonian political agenda, and if they did it would be to prevent rather than to promote progress. There is also a tendency to resort to threats and violence to resolve disputes rather than having a civil and respectful debate between two opposing parties. There have been a few recent instances of fist fights taking place during sessions of parliament and politicians punching journalists or threatening violence because of criticism.

    The country has had regular elections since its independence from Yugoslavia in 1991, but the only political entity with any governing experience at that time was the old communist party. The political establishment reconstituted as a leftist social democrat party and went on to dominate domestic politics for the next 14 years, winning in six out of the country's first seven democratic elections. Using their insider knowledge, leaders of the social democrats abruptly purchased newly denationalized industries for pennies on the dollar and shifted control of the private sector to their personal friends, just as their counterparts did throughout Eastern Europe after the fall of communism. A small number of connected political elites became millionaires seemingly overnight as they pocketed the profits from selling off national assets. In the meantime, factories were closed and unemployment rose sharply. That sort of crony capitalism created resentment and skepticism among large swaths of the electorate and set the country on an economic course that has proven difficult to derail.

    Weary of cronyism and the lack of progress that they were experiencing under the social democrats, many Macedonians enthusiastically opted to change course in 2006 by voting in the opposition. At the time, they were a center-right nationalist party who favored further political and economic integration with the West. For many the move was seen as a fresh start that would finally move the country past the baggage of the old system. The new government, headed by then 36-years-old Nikola Gruevski, promised to institute much needed reforms that would modernize the economy and finally bring prosperity. In his prior work as the minister of trade and then later as the minister of finance Gruevski had gained a positive reputation for openly embracing the principles of economic liberalism, such as free trade and low taxes. He had pushed to deregulate the economy and had overseen the process of restitution, by which the government returned properties confiscated by the communists to their original owners. He also cracked down on the cozy relationship between the business sector and certain politicians that was costing the government millions of dollars in dodged taxes.

Building on the strength of his lofty rhetoric and promise of economic reforms, Gruevski enjoyed widespread support early in his tenure. Young people welcomed his views on European integration, and there was even real optimism that Macedonia would soon join the European Union. He appealed to the populist segment of his base by continuing to live in his own personal apartment near downtown in a nice but unremarkable building instead of in the more lavish official residence. And the nationalists appreciated his stubbornly defiant position on the sensitive "Macedonian Question," which dates all the way back to 19th and early 20th century conflicts over territory and national identity in the Balkans. The matter is still not settled, and continues to have political consequences well into the 21st century.

The conflicts began when European nationalism was reaching extreme levels and the Ottoman Empire was in the process of collapsing. Greeks, Bulgarians, and Serbs fought to control the ethnically diverse Macedonian territory that the Ottomans had administered for the preceding five hundred years. Each side believed they had a rightful and historical claim, and therefore should be able to impose its national identity upon the inhabitants. After a series of bloody conflicts in what became a prelude to World War I, all three sides made out with some portion of the territory, the largest of which went to Greece. Many Slavic speaking Macedonians were stranded on the other side of a newly created international border in an era of ascendant Greek nationalism and were subsequently expelled from Greece or forced to assimilate. Quite a few elderly people still speak of their origins in Aegean Macedonia to this day, including Gruevski himself, whose grandparents fled the region.

When Yugoslavia administered the territory for the better part of the 20th century the issue was temporarily put to rest, but the emergence of the independent Republic of Macedonia in 1991 reopened the Macedonian Question. The Bulgarians take issue with the legitimacy of modern Macedonia's claim to King Samuel, whose empire controlled much of the Balkans prior to the Byzantines. From their perspective, the historical territory he controlled was part of the First Bulgarian Empire, and the cultural legacy of that empire is the rightful inheritance of the modern Bulgarian people. Macedonians counter that since his seat of power was in Skopje, the modern Macedonian capital, and was then moved to Ohrid, also in modern Macedonia, he is a Macedonian historical figure. For what it's worth, most historians maintain that self-conscious nationalism was an invention of late 19th century, rendering it highly unlikely that figures from the middle ages used or even understood ethnicity in the way we do today. But something tells me that partisans on either side are not especially interested in that.

Significantly, the cultural legacy of the territory includes claims to Saints Cyril and Methodius, known for creating the Cyrillic alphabet so they could translate the Bible to Slavic languages and spread Christianity to the Balkan Slavs. They were born in Thessaloniki, which is part of modern-day Greece, but they worked largely in what historians refer to as the Bulgarian Empire, whose administrative seat was first in modern-day Macedonia. Also in dispute are the true origins of more modern revolutionary heroes like Goce Delcev and Yane Sandanski who fought against the Ottomans for independence. Even though they fought for the independence of the territory named Macedonia, some scholars maintain that they saw themselves as Bulgarians. Balkan history, I guess it is safe to say, is complicated and fraught with tension.

These disputes may seem like petty squabbling, but they are important in the sense that they either lend credence to the legitimacy of Macedonian nationhood or undermine it completely, depending on which historical argument you accept. Quite a few scholars and politicians in modern Bulgaria argue that Macedonians have no legitimate claim to the territory or to those historical figures because Macedonians are a mere subset of Bulgarians and not a true nation unto themselves. Likewise, they argue that the mutually intelligible Macedonian language is a Bulgarian dialect and not a separate language. To drive this point home, the Bulgarian government offers European Union passports to Macedonians who will swear to an affidavit that they are in fact Bulgarian. Eager to get access to employment in much higher paying countries of the West, many Macedonians have swallowed their pride and signed on the dotted line.

While the disagreement with Bulgaria may be irksome to politicians and partisan academics, the ongoing dispute with Greece is far more acrimonious and has much farther reaching implications. Greece claims that the use of the name "Macedonia" reflects the irredentist intentions of slavophones to reclaim the territory's historical geographic extent. According to the Greek government, the name falsely suggests an association with Alexander the Great's ancient kingdom, which they argue has no relationship to the Slavic speaking Macedonians of the present, although both sides see him as their ethnic ancestor. The distinction matters to those involved because historical figures inform national identity and bolster claims to territory by way of the "we were here first" argument, just as it does in the Bulgaria dispute. The debate is so politically charged that the Gruevski administration objects to the use of the term "Slavic Macedonian" because it implies that there is another type of Macedonian, namely the Greek type. They barely even refer to Greece by name, calling it "our southern neighbor" instead. It's the Balkans. Things like this are as routine as they are complicated.

Perhaps in anticipation of the naming issue heating up, Thessaloniki, the second-largest city in Greece, renamed its airport the Macedonia International Airport in 1992, not even a year after the fall of Yugoslavia. The Greek government then pressured the newly independent Republic of Macedonia to change its flag, which Greece claimed appropriated the Vergina Sun, a cultural symbol that is also in use in its own Macedonian territories. Greece further stipulated that the country was to be officially accepted into the United Nations as the Former Yugoslav Republic of Macedonia (FYROM); a move that nearly all ethnic Macedonians strongly resent. Although many European countries and the United States now recognize the country as the Republic of Macedonia, Greece continually uses its veto power to block its accession into NATO and the European Union under that name. As recently as one year prior to the time of this writing Greek border officials were placing stickers that read "The Sign MK Is Not Recognized By Greece" on any car entering the country with a license plate using that abbreviation. Politics is everything, and everything is politics, including history, identity, names, territory, and license plates.

While his political predecessors showed a willingness to negotiate with Greece, and were even responsible for accepting the provisional name change to FYROM, Gruevski has depicted himself as a steadfast patriot who will never compromise on the "naming issue." He has openly engaged in a rhetorical war with

Greece over what his administration portrays as the right to self-determination. A mere four months into his tenure as prime minister the government announced plans to rename Skopje's international airport to Alexander the Great, despite the existence of an airport with the same name nearby in Greece. A few years later they christened the Alexander the Great Highway, which is the main road leading from the airport to the Greek border. Not long after that they named the newly remodeled national stadium after Phillip the Second, Alexander the Great's father.

Greece took those moves as unnecessary provocations, but they were especially aggrieved in 2010 when the Gruevski administration revealed plans to make Skopje into a veritable urban theme park dedicated to Alexander and his entire family. Part of the plan was to erect an 80-foot bronze statue of "an equestrian warrior" that strongly resembles a monument to Alexander the Great in Thessaloniki, although the latter version stands at only 20 feet tall. On the other side of the central plaza is a 95-foot statue of a "warrior with accompanying elements" that looks a lot like Philip the Second gazing at his son's monument from afar with his fist raised victoriously in the air. On the walk from one oversized monument to the other one can also pass by sculptures of Alexander's mother depicted in the different stages of motherhood.

The statues are actually just one component of a much larger project known as Skopje 2014. On the surface, the overall goal of the project was to modernize the look and feel of the capital. Prior to its current facelift the downtown had a distinctly socialist aesthetic, primarily because nearly all of the buildings were constructed after the devastating earthquake of 1963 when Yugoslavia was responsible for the recovery effort. Skopje 2014 was supposed to be a long overdue urban renewal project that would beautify the city and make it more attractive to tourists and residents alike. But as more details of the project's full scope started to surface, it became clear that its creators had larger ambitions than simple renovation. Whereas Skopje 1963 bore the heavy architectural imprint of Yugoslavia, which actively suppressed ethnic nationalism, the architecture of Skopje 2014 would reflect the true national identity of the Macedonian people.

In the place of boxy concrete structures there are now buildings with white columns and domes flanked by sculptures and monuments to heroes of the past, disputed identities and all. The purpose of the old socialist architecture was to convey statist authority, but the new façade draws heavily on the imagery of antiquity and conveys a narrative of continuity from the ancient past to the present. That, anyway, was the plan.

The result has been a bizarre pastiche of incongruous buildings and monuments that have had the unintended consequence of making Skopje the kitsch capital of Europe. Oversized monuments and dozens of oddly-placed statues sit awkwardly next a replica of the Arc De Triomphe, and in the near future there will be a Ferris wheel modeled on the Eye of London. Along the banks of the Vardar River, which functions as the de facto boundary between the Albanian (Muslim) side of town and the Macedonian (Orthodox) side, is a row of brand new governmental buildings rendered in the Palladian style of architecture. The all-white structures have hollow columns and noticeably cheap facades that would not be out of place in Las Vegas. Out in the river sit three faux Spanish galleons resembling pirate ships that function as stationary restaurants and cafes, even though the boats themselves block the view of the new buildings on the other side of the river. The various architectural styles and haphazard placement of the monuments look like a game of Sim City gone wrong, except that it is very much real life.

The Skopje 2014 project endeared the Gruevski administration to the populist and nationalist segments of his political base, but it has been deeply controversial, and not just because of its crimes against architectural decency. The total cost, estimated at over five percent of the national GDP, seemed at odds with Gruevski's self-cultivated image as having a shrewd economic mind. Many wonder if that money may have been better spent on the country's infrastructure or on its underfunded public healthcare and education systems. Worse still, the national unemployment rate stayed at over 30 percent for the duration of his tenure, wages remained stagnant, and politicization in the workplace continued as before. Depending on who you talk to, many things have actually gotten worse since he took office. There were also accusations that lucrative construction contracts for Skopje 2014 were steered to friends and family of the administration. Different band, same song.

In most democracies, administrations often find it difficult, if not impossible, to survive a combination of staggering unemployment, financial mismanagement, allegations of a return to crony capitalism, and derision from the international community. The Gruevski administration not only survived, but stayed in power for over a decade, longer than any previous administration since the country's independence. Part of his unlikely resilience comes from his willingness to take on the many nationalist grievances that the Macedonian people genuinely feel. They have been on Europe's doorstep for decades now, but veto after veto over the naming issue with Greece has stymied any progress. But a more important factor, and one that also contributes to the lack of progress of towards Europe, is his ruthless suppression of the media.

In 2005, the year before Gruevski took office, the independent media watchdog Reporters Without Borders ranked Macedonia's freedom of the press 43rd out of 167 countries, one spot ahead of the United States. It was considered a success story among post-socialist countries and taken as a sign of democratic progress. Pro-democracy reforms were implemented as a condition of gaining European Union candidacy in the early 2000s and the country seemed to be heading on a positive course. By 2010, four years into Gruevski's reign, the ranking slid to 68th and Macedonia joined its Balkan neighbors in an authoritarian turn, prompting concern from the watchdog organization and from the European Union alike.

As it turns out, their concerns were justified, because the following year special police forces stormed a television station that had been critical of the government and jailed its owner. The raid had symbolic significance because the station, named A1, was the first private channel to broadcast in the country when it opened in 1993, and was still its most popular domestic channel at the time of the raid. The central news had grown increasingly critical of the administration and started exposing numerous instances of government malfeasance. Under the pretense that the owner had failed to pay taxes, the Gruevski administration shut the station down completely and forced three affiliated newspapers out of print. The owner remains in jail as of 2016. Those actions had a chilling effect on all national media and set a distinct tone: dissent will not be tolerated, either get on message, or we will close you down.

After the A1 raid, owners friendly with the government took control of every Macedonian language media outlet in the country except for one, dropping its 2014 ranking to 123, ahead of only Belarus, Russia, and Ukraine in terms of their European peers. Moderate reforms in the face of international criticism helped its ranking improve to 118 by 2016, which now places Macedonia alongside Nigeria, Qatar, the United Arab Emirates, and Afghanistan in terms of press freedom. Even during a rightward and authoritarian shift in Eastern European politics more generally, the Gruevski administration in Macedonia stands out as an aggressive suppressor of free speech.

Administration officials directly feed talking points to the news, painting a picture of internal strength, stability, and even prosperity. Leery of losing their job, journalists self-censor by avoiding topics that could be seen as criticism. During election season media owners refuse to run opposition ads, mostly out of fear of government retribution. It is not uncommon for progovernment ads to occupy every available commercial slot in the run up to an election, and some ads can last as long as five minutes. Television stations favorably cover staged rallies and protests, where card-carrying party members are compelled to show up and in some cases even to check-in on Facebook to show how much support the party has. Failure to do so will result in the loss of a job or getting passed over for a promotion in cases were firing is not feasible.

The whole charade is a cynical ploy to make it seem as if the administration has widespread support. Any criticism of the government that does manage to make it to the news is explained away as propaganda from unnamed "foreign enemies" or "foreign agencies" that are trying to destabilize Macedonia and create a permanent political crisis. Officials decline to say which foreign countries are involved and what their goals are, but everyone understands that implication as code for the CIA and to a lesser extent Western European intelligence agencies. They also see NGOs and anything funded by George Soros, a liberal figure who invests in free media projects in post-socialist countries, as potentially dangerous forces with questionable intentions.

At least to a certain segment of the population, all of these tactics have been shockingly effective. The older generation already harbors a latent suspicion of the West, and they are more than willing to consume the narrative that malicious foreign agencies have it in for Macedonia. Many are steadfast in their belief that those same organizations being called out today broke up Yugoslavia, and they have yet to taste the prosperity and stability that was supposed to follow. In addition, the Balkans have been in the midst of an international political tug of war for generations now, causing many people to put up their guard against anything that comes across as unwanted meddling. For the administration and the media it controls, "foreign agencies" are the low-hanging fruit that cloud any debate and insert enough doubt to keep the opposition at bay.

Ruthless suppression of the media also shields the government from scrutiny over its antics during elections. One such antic is to get local party bosses to make a list of people who "owe" them votes in return for employment or some other service. When the results come out, they compare the difference between the votes received and votes expected. In the smaller communities, it is possible to attribute any deviations from votes expected to specific individuals and then take retribution by firing them or their relatives from jobs that the party connection helped set up in the first place. In other communities, people who have been deceased for years or who emigrated long ago are still on the voter registry, and their "votes" can sometimes help put a ruling party candidate over the top.

In districts with a higher concentration of voters who favor the opposition, the administration employs a variety of means to suppress voter turnout. On a recent election day, for example, the electricity went out in the parts of Skopje that were expected to vote for the opposition. Many of the apartment buildings in those districts are between eight and ten stories, so the people who live on higher floors, and especially the elderly and disabled, mostly stayed home when they saw that the elevators did not work. Rumors were flying that the ruling party cut the power on purpose to minimize competition at the ballot box. The average person in the Balkans loves a good conspiracy theory, so I mostly dismissed those fears and assumed it was just a coincidence. A few weeks later, leaked recordings emerged in which officials from the ruling party were actually talking to each other about how they had, in fact, cut the power on purpose to minimize turnout.

Those recordings were just a small part of much larger wiretapping scandal that included thousands of hours of recorded conversations between members of the administration, including Gruevski and his most senior cabinet members. The tapes exposed, among other things, numerous instances of blatant electoral fraud, deep political intervention in the judicial system, and plans to cover up a murder for which a government security detail was directly responsible. Unsurprisingly, the government blamed unnamed "foreign agencies" for the recordings, and suggested that the voices had been spliced together from other recordings to fabricate quotes and even whole conversations. The recordings did lead to the resignation of a few top officials, and Gruevski himself stepped down from power a year later, but thus far no one involved is in prison. Instead, there have been attempts to charge the opposition party members who made the recordings public with crimes against the state.

Even though Gruevski has officially stepped down at the time of this writing, the party that he shaped in his image is still in power, and ten years of increasingly authoritarian rule has taken its toll. A dark cloud of pessimism permeates nearly every transaction and every conversation. Fear, oppression, and in some cases violence towards the opposition now characterize the politics of a country that was making real progress towards joining the European Union just ten years ago. Macedonia is now more politically isolated and further away from Europe than at any point in its brief post-independence history. For many young people who are looking for a different way forward, the best option is to go abroad, beyond the reach of the country's political system.

As badly as these events have damaged hopes that the country can continue to transition from the old ways, there are positive signs that things can improve. The arrival of low-cost airlines has significantly increased the country's access to Western Europe, and many locals can now afford to travel to places that were once prohibitively expensive. An entire generation of young people is venturing beyond the confines of the southeastern Balkan region on student exchanges and work-and-travel programs; something that the older generation rarely did. They bring back with them new desires and viewpoints on politics and the functioning of democracy, opening up a substantial generation gap between those who mostly grew up in Yugoslavia and those who were born slightly before or after its breakup. Those who want to go in a different direction have taken to the streets in protest after protest, and in some cases have endured beatings from the police and assaults from counter protesters.

There is also a healthy selection of satirical political news programs modeled on *The Daily Show* that use social media to bypass the government's control. And a combination of public outcry and international pressure have forced the government to backtrack on some of its most egregious abuses. All of these developments signal an appetite for change and a willingness to work for progress rather than to passively accept the status quo. They also illustrate the extent to which democracy, an institution so vaunted upon its arrival over 25 years ago, is still very much a work in progress.

CHAPTER 8

The New Macedonian Question

Macedonia is such a small country that its significance is easy to overlook. At the time of this writing, if you search on Amazon for books about travel in Europe, you will find subcategories for Andorra, Estonia, Greenland, Liechtenstein, and pretty much every other European country, large and small... except for Macedonia. Aside from people with Macedonian citizenship, or perhaps those with Macedonian or Albanian heritage, getting people to care about what goes on there may be a hard sell. Yet for all that it lacks in size and international reputation, its geopolitical significance can hardly be understated, and the direction that the country takes can have far reaching implications on many, many pressing issues of the 21st century. It is easy to forget, after all, that just over one hundred years ago events in the Balkans largely set the course for how the 20th century unfolded in Europe, which in turn drew in much of the rest of the world. Although it is impossible to state with any certainty how the remainder of the 21st century will play out in Macedonia, there are at least three concurrent, interrelated phenomena that are highly likely to influence the trajectory of events in the decades to come.

First, Macedonia's future will increasingly be characterized by its changing demographics. Not only does it have one of the lowest fertility rates in Europe, the country has been experiencing a sustained outmigration of its young people for over a decade. At the very least, in the near future there will be fewer young people in the workforce paying into state healthcare and pension plans and a higher percentage of aging retirees leaving the workforce to draw on those benefits. At worst, a smaller nation like Macedonia, whose identity is already contested on political and ethnic grounds, may end up with too few people to be a viable state in its current form. That is not to say that the country will cease to exist necessarily, but that a Macedonian state that looks after the interests of ethnic Macedonians may become difficult to manage.

To underscore the extent to which emigration affects the country, Macedonia and its non-EU border countries (Albania, Kosovo, and Serbia) joined Syria, Iraq, and Afghanistan as the top seven countries seeking asylum in Germany during the peak of the 2015 immigration and refugee crisis. While many of them were turned away as economic migrants, their presence on the list alongside refugees from those war torn hellscapes says a lot about how they perceive the future in their home countries. Ostensibly most people go for higher paying jobs, but there is also a strong desire to experience something new. In the past most people were simply unaware of all the opportunity and excitement of the outside world, but today it can hardly be avoided as images of new lifestyles and desires are splashed across screens at virtually all hours of the day. Most of those items are either unavailable or unattainable in Macedonia, pushing people to go satisfy their curiosity on work-and-travel programs or on cheap direct flights to the West with low-cost carriers.

In an attempt to offset population losses from massive emigration, the Macedonian government began introducing financial incentives to encourage women to have more children as of 2008. If a woman has a third child (*treto dete*), she will receive a monthly payment of 8,000 denars (around 150 USD) for the first ten years of the child's life. Since many people live on less than 400 dollars a month, the financial incentive is attractive enough to at least merit consideration, although anecdotally I do not know a single person under the age of 40 who has more than two children. In addition to the cultural belief that having two children is "normal," women are expected to work outside the home while still taking on the bulk of domestic duties, which limits the appeal of having a large family for many women. Plus, even having one child can be such a financial burden that many people are now putting off having a second, much less a third.

To promote the "third child" policy, the government has financed a public relations campaign called "Create the Future." The ads are placed in virtually every commercial slot during high-profile sporting events that air on the state-run Macedonian Radio and Television channel (MRT1) to maximize exposure.

Careful to downplay the financial considerations that influence family planning, the commercials indirectly promote the *treto dete* policy by speaking to the cultural practice of equating emotional fulfillment with parenthood. This is not a uniquely Balkan tendency, to be sure. In the United States, for example, men and women who openly state they have no intentions of ever having children often face accusations of being "selfish, shallow, and self-absorbed," to borrow the title phrase from Megan Daum's collection of essays on the subject.

At the same time, the idea that having children is a choice has gained widespread acceptance in the West, especially among those with higher education and demanding professions. For many people in the Balkans, by contrast, kids and family are an automatic part of life, not a choice that people make. Having children, but especially sons, is how you validate your womanhood or manhood. In my own experience, people seem emotionally hurt when I tell them that some of my American friends never plan to have kids. I get the impression they view that decision as something like a mental pathology that they just can't understand and not like a rational choice that has been carefully considered. The minute-long commercials draw heavily on that cultural practice, as the message at the end literally spells out on the screen:

"Children are our joy, our wealth. They are the foundation of the family. In creating new life, we are closer to God. Our tradition of having many children in the family is our future. For a happy family, for a secure future, increase your family. Have a third child."

In one commercial, a man who appears to be in his early sixties is seen flipping through a family photo album. As he looks at an old photo of what the viewer assumes are his ancestors, he says that his great grandmother raised seven children during two wars. He turns the page to a somewhat smaller family and says that his grandmother raised five children, also during wartime, even though one more mouth to feed meant that others would have to go a little hungry. He turns the page again to show a slightly smaller family and explains that he has three siblings, who despite not having many possessions, never lacked for anything. He continues turning the pages of the album, each time with fewer people in the photos, while stating that today's young people are waiting to get their lives in order before having children. Finally, he gets to the last page, where there is no photo at all, and just in case the message was not clear already, he spells it out for you:

"Those of us who are approaching the end of the road do not have much time left," he says directly into the camera. "We want to feel the joy of having many grandchildren, and to be sure that someone will continue our family line... Everything passes," he assures, "including your career and worries and problems. Family is the most important." This message, of course, is a way to skirt the financial reasons people often cite for not having more children by essentially saying, "We know it's tough out there, things used to be even tougher and people still had large families. Push through and start having more kids now, or our people will disappear just like the photos in this album."

On the surface, the *treto dete* policy and its accompanying ad push appear to be a response to the grim mathematics of life tables. If fertility rates do not increase soon, more people will die than are being born, and the population of what is already one of Europe's smallest countries will get even smaller. As is the case with many things in the Balkans, however, nationalist concerns and the weight of history linger in the background of the policy. The fact that the advertisements are only produced in Macedonian language is a not so subtle indication of the type of future the campaign has in mind. While all citizens of the country are entitled to its benefits, the implicit goal is to increase the fertility of ethnic Macedonians, who currently comprise around 66 percent of the national population. That percentage is projected to fall in the near future, and considering the tepid response to the *treto dete* policy thus far, the drop could be rather considerable in a few decades.

Albanians, who tend to have larger families, will see their share of the population rise from its current level of 25 percent, and it is not inconceivable that they could comprise half of the population in two generations time. The specter of losing majority status and ceding political power to a rival group is worrisome to some ethnic Macedonians, to say the least.

Those worries are not unfounded. A vocal minority of the Albanian population within Macedonia, Albania, and Kosovo has expressed a desire to form Greater Albania, which would include a significant section of western Macedonia as well as Skopje. If Albanians were to become Macedonia's majority ethnic group, it is quite likely that those calls would grow louder as the cause gains political momentum. Considering Europe's fragile unity and the increasing frequency of similar calls for secessionism in the United Kingdom, Spain, and Ukraine, the shifting demographic situation has real potential to destabilize the Balkans once again.

Second, the demographic concerns feed into the growing levels of militant nationalism that have plagued former Yugoslavia off and on since its collapse. Except for a brief period of clashes between Albanian insurgents and government forces in 2001, Macedonia has mostly managed to avoid the sort of armed confrontations seen in Bosnia, Croatia, Serbia, and Kosovo. But ethnic tensions simmer just below the surface, and those tensions occasionally boil over into riots and clashes in the street. Animosities have only increased during the Gruevski administration, in part because of a deliberate push to replace the Yugoslav idea of civic nationalism with a return to ethno-nationalism. Whereas civic nationalism is largely based on devotion to the state's philosophical goals, ethno-nationalism emphasizes the unique cultural aspects that supposedly inform the national character, often at the expense of other cultures that may also be present.

The historical pretext of the Skopje 2014 project is the most obvious example of that shift, but the government has also actively and enthusiastically promoted Orthodox Christianity as a central component of Macedonian national identity. There are now eleven state holidays in Macedonia, including Christmas Day (January 7), Easter Monday, Saints Cyril and Methodius Day, and Saint Clement of Ohrid Day from the Orthodox Christian calendar. There are an additional five non-working religious holidays that only apply to Orthodox Christians, although the state does now recognize the final day of Ramadan as an official state holiday and permits the various religious and ethnic minorities to have one additional non-working holiday. Yugoslavia, by contrast, had four state holidays a year, none of which came from any religious calendar.

In part, the government's embrace of Orthodox Christianity reflects a broader religious awakening taking place throughout post-socialist Eastern Europe. As governments allow more political freedom to openly practice religion, there has been a gradual rise in interest among the public. Protestant and Mormon missionaries, mostly from the United States, are a common sight in Macedonia, and young people are more likely to view Orthodox Christianity as a central aspect of their personal identity than their parents would.

The newfound religious consciousness is also a form of pushback against the tidal wave of cultural change that hit Eastern Europe once it opened up to the West. I was told many times that westernization was responsible for a deterioration in morals and that it brought new vices like sports gambling and drinking; even if those were already present. At least for some people, the church (or the mosque) acts as a symbolic buffer against the outside world and helps preserve the traditional values that they feel are slipping away.

As earnest as those sentiments may be, the government's appeals to ethno-nationalism signal a troubling breakdown of the separation between church and state in one of Europe's most ethnically and religiously diverse countries. Not only has the government firmly placed its institutional support behind Orthodox Christianity, the church has the overt financial support of the state as well. In the past few years alone there have been dozens of new churches constructed in the municipality of Aerodrom, which is the most ethnically homogenous Macedonian administrative district in Skopje. Although the stated purpose of the church construction boom is to give the citizens a chance to express their ethnic heritage, it is widely understood as a message to Albanians that Aerodrom is a "clean" neighborhood, and they are not welcome. It is common parlance, by the way, to use the term "clean" in reference to ethnic composition, as uncomfortable as that sounds in English because of its association with the term ethnic cleansing. The municipality also erected a giant cross just outside of a Turkish-funded apartment complex in Aerodrom amid speculation that the owners would be amenable to Albanian tenants, although officials deny those accusations.

These moves have further alienated the Albanian community, particularly the younger generation who has come of age under very different circumstances from their parents. They were young children during the 1999 war in Kosovo and the subsequent 2001 conflict in Macedonia. In their lifetimes Albanians have vocally agitated for equal rights and social justice, and ethnic identities have hardened. Unlike their parents, they attended schools segregated by ethnicity and are less likely to learn Macedonian language or to even engage with Macedonian society. They grew up in a time when ethnicity and nationality shifted from being defined as an internal construct to one that is in opposition to the "other."

Their parents in Yugoslavia may have been nominally Muslim, but they grew up with a secular and tolerant form of Islam. Very few women from the older generation cover their hair, and the men rarely have beards. The halal diet is only loosely followed, if at all, and alcohol is not a strict taboo. Many people over the age of 40, especially if they grew up in an urbanized area, have never even been inside a mosque. They may celebrate a few Islamic holidays with traditions left over from the Ottoman period, but they are mostly unaware of anything beyond basic religious doctrine; not unlike their Macedonian counterparts.

Many from the new generation, by contrast, take a far more rigid stance on religion. Young Albanian ladies are much more likely to cover their hair and to dress modestly than their mothers, and some of the more conservative women refuse to shake hands with men, even their relatives. Likewise, an increasing number of young Albanian men grow beards and carry prayer beads as an outward expression of religious devotion. They attend the mosque more frequently and study the Koran and other religious writings more diligently. Some of the more ardent Albanians have even pushed back against the celebration of New Year, which they resent for its incorporation of western Christmas imagery.

Since their parents are less likely to be observant, and many of the older imams adhere to the relaxed form of Islam that was common in Yugoslavia, young people often turn to the internet to engage with other Muslims from more religiously conservative countries in the Middle East. They also interact with clerics and Islamic scholars from places like Qatar and the UAE at cultural centers and religious agencies sponsored by wealthy individuals from the Gulf states. Some of those same people finance the construction of impressive new mosques with towering white minarets and neon lights; a marked contrast in style from the more reserved and understated Ottoman aesthetic. This increased engagement with the Middle East, both online and in person, allows young people to learn more about the Islamic belief system and its tenets, but it also has introduced the younger generation to the far stricter Wahhabist ideology and pushed them further away from the moderate role that religion has traditionally played in the society.

Of much greater concern is the fact that hundreds, if not thousands of Albanians from Kosovo and Macedonia have fled to Syria to join the so-called Islamic State. Kosovo, in fact, has provided the highest per capita number of Islamic State fighters from Europe thus far. This is a disturbing trend on many levels, and portends a profound social change in an ardently pro-American Muslim country where a giant statue of Bill Clinton adorns the capital city. There is also the looming prospect that experienced fighters may return home from the conflict in Syria and continue their violent struggle in a society that has grown more receptive to their ideology. For the moment, these are only hypothetical hazards that may or may not be on the horizon. But failure to monitor the situation more closely, coupled with the continued inability of the European Union to coordinate a response to the refugee crisis, could have serious ramifications in the near future.

The third event that is currently playing out in Macedonia is whether the country should further pursue integration with the West or foster deeper ties with Russia and its allies. Similar questions are facing many of the other remaining countries that have yet to join the European Union, such as Serbia, Montenegro, and most notably Ukraine. Macedonia was firmly on course for further integration with the West until quite recently. Talks of joining the European Union and NATO were progressing, and it seemed for a time that only the name issue with Greece was standing in its way. But media suppression, rising ethno-nationalism, and a refusal to make basic democratic reforms have taken Macedonia down an authoritarian path, and subsequently dampened its prospects of joining the West.

Russia, on the other hand, presents a strongly contrasting approach to governance and international relations that has been well-suited to the Gruevski administration. Whereas the West has been critical of Macedonia's undemocratic turn, Russia has been willing to overlook domestic matters as long as business is good. The Gruevski administration has a very cozy relationship with Russian billionaire Sergei Samsonenko, who purchased the country's most high-profile handball and soccer teams. Samsonenko was given a prime real estate deal to build a gaudy Russian Orthodox Church, a new handball arena in which his team plays, and a small but chic hotel called, aptly enough, Hotel Russia. Macedonia is also in the path of the proposed South

Stream pipeline designed to carry gas from Russia through Turkey and southeastern Europe, and stands to benefit immensely if the project is ever realized. Lukoil, the largest oil company in Russia, is already a major presence in the country. And as of 2016 it was announced that Macedonia would work to increase Russian tourism by eventually creating airline connections between the two countries. The relationship between Macedonia and Russia, as these business deals suggest, is strong and set to get even stronger.

In many ways the burgeoning alliance is a natural fit. Russia was the first major country to officially recognize the preferred name of the Republic of Macedonia shortly after its independence, and even before that Yugoslavia had an amicable relationship with the Soviet Union because of their shared political philosophy. In the past there were schools and other public projects named after Soviet heroes like Lenin, and many roads still bear their names. I lived on Yuri Gagarin street, for example, during my time in Skopje. Russia is also a standard bearer of the Slavic cultural identity and very much sees itself as the protector of Orthodox Christians throughout Europe.

More recently, there has been a marked turn towards Putin and his style of politics. Many Macedonians admire what he has been able to accomplish in Russia, and they are especially fond of his tough rhetoric against his political adversaries and the West. For some, it recalls the good old days in Yugoslavia when there was another world power that could stand up to the demands and political pressure of the United States and its allies. They also appreciate the Russian approach to international affairs, which maintains that the conflicts in Bosnia and Kosovo, no matter how violent, were domestic matters in which outsiders had no right to intervene.

    The Kremlin has been more than willing to support the Gruevski administration's claims that Macedonia's political problems are the work of foreign agents (read: CIA and the European Union) trying destabilize the country, which has resonated well with the nationalist base. In return the Gruevski administration has been happy to allow its own media to regurgitate Russian talking points on everything from the crisis in Ukraine to corruption in Washington to the ineptness of the European Union. Most of what passes for news these days, especially on the internet portals from which most Macedonians get their information, are simply stories copied from pro-Russian websites and translated directly into Macedonian without even bothering to question the source. Domestic investigative reporting can be dangerous, and international reports critical of the government are dismissed as evidence of "foreign bias" or "propaganda" or "western brainwashing," no matter how credible the source is. The collective influence of that media strategy has won Putin many fans in Macedonia, and has successfully chipped away at the political will to attempt further integration with the West.

The recent pro-Putin, and by extension, pro-Russia turn is emblematic of the love-hate relationship that many Macedonians have with the United States and the West more generally. On the one hand, they have experienced the raw political and military power of the United States and actively despise its foreign policy. The NATO bombing of Serbia and war in Kosovo laid the groundwork for the 2001 conflict in Macedonia, and opened the door for an expanded American presence in the Balkans. There is now a permanent American military base in Kosovo, and the American embassy in Skopje is by far the largest foreign diplomatic complex in the country, if not the region. Macedonians feel that their own government has been too acquiescent to American political demands, and are especially resentful of the sense of empowerment that American support has afforded Albanians. Russia presents an unapologetically pro-Slavic, pro-Orthodox alternative to that form of governance, and that is an appealing prospect for Macedonians who have felt overwhelmed by western influence and intervention.

On the other hand, it is difficult to find a family that does not have an immediate relative who lives in the United States, and there is an insatiable desire for American cultural products. Young people are completely up to date with American television shows, movies, and music. They update their

Facebook status is English almost as frequently as in Macedonian, and kids sing "happy birthday to you" at their friends' parties. I even know some grandparents who complained to me that their grandchildren understand Macedonian perfectly well, but because they watch so much American television they prefer to speak a mixture of English and Macedonian, even though they have never lived abroad. Nearly everyone I know applies for the immigrant diversity lottery each year in the hopes of getting a green card, and quite a few overstay their tourist visas and live in the United States illegally. I know of zero people in Macedonia, by contrast, who have even visited Russia, much less tried to move there, legally or not.

    The direction Macedonia ultimately chooses will largely determine what type of country it wants to be in the near future. Both sides, it should be said, have their respective advantages and disadvantages. Pursuing integration with the West will likely bring more economic opportunities and increase the country's market access, and it may eventually lead to inclusion in the visa-free work and travel agreement that most of Europe currently enjoys. There would likely be more transparency in the government and more freedom in the media, and the government would have to take more serious steps to ensure that future elections are free and fair. Western integration would necessitate some cultural concessions that people may have been loath to grant thus far, such as working towards a more inclusive society in which Albanians and other minorities have far more status than they do now.

Those all sound good in theory, but the political climate in Europe has already started pushing back against the tide of immigrants coming from newly admitted countries like Romania and Bulgaria. There is no guarantee that Macedonia's attempts to integrate will be reciprocated, and decades of economic globalization in the developing world have brought mixed results of which people are well aware. Furthermore, joining NATO and aligning itself with American foreign policy would mean that the Macedonian government lends tacit, and in some cases active support for future military endeavors like the one in Kosovo, despite political or even moral opposition.

Casting their lot with Russia has its own set of advantages and disadvantages. On the positive side, at least from a certain perspective, Russia is unlikely to be involved in domestic politics. Macedonia would be free to continue upon its ethno-nationalist path unobstructed, and there would be essentially no pushback over media suppression or democratic reforms. In that way, the will of the people would be respected, although whether or not one agrees with that logic is a matter of political philosophy. Macedonia would also be a destination for increased Russian investments as it seeks to expand its area of influence, which could bring prosperity in a way that the West has failed to do thus far. On the other hand, sinking further into ethno-nationalist tendencies will almost certainly bring sanctions from the West, and could isolate Macedonia even further. It could also give the government leeway to seek reprisals against Albanians and to walk back some of the civil rights advances that have been achieved since the 2001 conflict.

The way in which Macedonia chooses to respond to these three challenges will undoubtedly have a tremendous impact on the regional stability of the Balkans, still one of Europe's most sensitive fault lines. With perhaps the exception of Bosnia, no other Balkan country faces the unique challenge of simultaneously managing a demographic crisis, rising religious extremism, and growing international pressure to choose sides. Add in the country's role in the ongoing refugee crisis and the ascendancy of Islamist politics in nearby Turkey, and it is easy to see why the fate of Macedonia, despite its small size, is as important now as it was when the Macedonian Question was first posed over a century ago.

PART III

On Leaving

CHAPTER 9

The Next New Beginning

After living in Macedonia for almost exactly three years and one month, my wife and I moved back to the United States, and have since said goodbye to our friends and family there. As hard as that decision was, in many ways it is emblematic of the problems currently facing the country. Both of us wanted to live there, and we both had decent jobs. Contrary to what most locals expected, I actually liked my life there, in large part because it was so easy to make friends and pass the time enjoyably. We lived across the street from a modern supermarket, our balcony overlooked a verdant city park, and we could walk to downtown in ten minutes. In most American cities those amenities would make rent unaffordable, but we paid less than two hundred dollars a month. I took a big risk moving there and jumped right in to the culture, and in return almost everyone I met embraced me from the first day. In the beginning we planned to stay there indefinitely and build a future, despite the fact that so many people our age were desperate to get out and live abroad. For some time, at least, everything was going well.

But before too long, the reality that pushes so many people to move abroad began catching up to us. It started off relatively small, like becoming increasingly annoyed by the general lack of kindness to strangers, or growing weary of the cloud of negativity that characterizes basic conversation. As that atmosphere started to rub off on me, I developed a sense a pessimism, skepticism, and suspicion that I never had before. I first noticed that demeanor in my wife when we met in the United States, long before I had any plans to ever visit the Balkans, much less live there. I took my computer to the Apple Store for service and when they took it behind the counter and to a back room, she seemed visibly angry and ready to chase after them. Confused, I asked her what the problem was, and she told me that I should not let some stranger take my computer to a different room where I can't see what they are doing because they will probably open it up, take out the new parts, and replace them with used parts. Back then I thought that was hilarious, especially at the Apple Store, where superior customer service entices people to pay more for products that they could get for far less money elsewhere.

    Living in Macedonia taught me to see things from her perspective, and now I completely know where she was coming from, because that is very likely what would happen there. Now that I have seen how things can be, I can't help but have the same doubts and suspicions. Whereas many Americans have a naïve sense of optimism and trust, Balkan people are skeptical and always on the lookout for the catch, almost in anticipation of being cheated or wronged in some way. Even though I have been back in the United States for over six months at this point, I continue to carry that burden of suspicion and skepticism with me. When I am out running, I am constantly surveying my surroundings for dogs that might attack me, or cars that might hit me, or strangers that might yell at me just because I have the temerity to exercise in their presence. I never even thought about doing those things before. I still can't get used to how friendly customer service workers are, and how smoothly basic errands can be accomplished with so little effort and in such a short amount of time.

At first I was shielded from the negative sides of the country because I was a foreigner who did not understand the language. But in the end, my desire to live like a local proved to be a double-edged sword. Foreigners from the West come to Macedonia with a certain set of hidden privileges. People go out of their way to make sure you are enjoying your time, in part because of the culture of hospitality, but also because they respect westerners, sometimes to an uncomfortable degree. That was made clear to me from the first day that I set foot in the country and my in-laws rolled out the red carpet, giving me more food and drink than I thought was possible and taking me all around the country. It was reinforced many times later, such as when I was at a restaurant with two American friends and my Macedonian wife. The waiter asked the three Americans what we would like to drink in English, but did not even bother to take my wife's order because he knew she was a local. Restaurants know that Americans have a habit of tipping if the waiters seem extra friendly, which is not customary in Macedonia. As a result, Americans and other westerners can get a vastly different picture of customer service and other forms of public treatment than a local would.

Furthermore, only a very small percentage of foreigners in Macedonia know the language, so they are mostly oblivious to the daily trials and tribulations that characterize life for so many people there. As the saying goes, ignorance is bliss. Although my attempt to integrate with the local culture was mostly successful and warmly received, I became acutely, even painfully aware of those daily hardships, and saw how things can be when people do not assume that you are a wealthy American ready to leave a nice tip or pay more for a service without asking any questions. By the same token, if keep your mouth shut and let a local person pay for the taxi or find you an apartment, you will get the local price, which can really save a lot of money.

Over time those relatively mundane aspects of living there developed into much more concrete anxieties. Looking ten or even five years into the future, it was not at all clear how my wife and I could ever improve our financial situation there without forging some powerful political ties. If anything we were going backwards because my salary was suddenly reduced by almost half with no warning and no explanation. We were also planning on having children, but I was concerned by the prevalence of outdated medical practices and poor state of the country's education system. Even the state-run daycare program, which is something sorely lacking in the United States, is fraught with overcrowding, underfunding, and a shortage of childcare professionals because of the tendency to hire people based on connections rather than experience or qualifications.

And then, the dog I brought from home and cared for since he was a puppy was attacked and killed by another dog right in front of our apartment, simply because the other owner did not feel like walking his large and aggressive dog with a leash. None of those things are unusual or even surprising there, and it became too difficult to ignore those disadvantages. I no longer felt the desire to tough things out in Macedonia when I didn't have to, and we followed the path that so many others have taken, and many more will take after us. If the extent of that trend was not clear to me already, it really came into focus when we took several large boxes of our clothes and shoes to the post office and shipped them to the United States. Without missing a beat, the postal worker put the boxes on the scale, and made a very matter of fact observation: "You're leaving." I wondered how many boxes like that she had shipped already.

I am completely aware that the United States is not a utopia free of any problems, and the decision to move back was not taken lightly. Living abroad for a few years allowed me to step back and see my home country from a new perspective, and put social issues like mass shootings, racial tension, and economic inequality into a new light. I knew they were there before, but it is easy to overlook their severity and social implications from the inside. That is especially true for a white middle-class person like myself who is largely insulated from the ill effects of those phenomena. I was also struck by how my friends and family in the United States keep each other at a distance in a way that Balkan people would never dream of. I had gotten used to the hospitality routines and the constant checking in. Even if that wasn't my style, it definitely gave me the feeling that someone cares and that I belonged. It may be difficult to get personal space in Macedonia, but finding company or help with basic tasks that life brings is not.

I had to come to terms with the fact that although childcare and healthcare may be more reliable and higher quality back home, it matters little if you cannot afford either one. When Macedonians hear about the relative lack of social and family resources in the United States, they are shocked at how heartless and barbaric it all sounds. Trying to explain to them why one of the richest countries in the world can't seem to find the political will to do a better job makes it even worse. I also gained a new sense of emptiness when I pass by the houses in the American suburbs that are so neat and orderly, with their manicured lawns and new cars in the garage, because there is a distinct lack of community compared to what you can find in

Macedonia. The food there is fresher, tastier, and cheaper, and you don't need a car to find a quality market or a grocery store that serves fresh and local food. Indeed, many of these points are exactly what Macedonian expats find difficult about living in the United States.

On the other hand, seeing how much of a struggle it can be to get ahead in Macedonia gave me a new appreciation for the plethora of opportunities that we have in the United States. I came back home with a new drive to take advantage of those opportunities now that I have a deeper sense of how many people in the world will never be in that position, no matter how hard they try. Whereas in Macedonia there were only limitations and a depressing lack of hope for anything better, my wife and I now have options and can make plans about how to improve our future prospects. Most importantly, we have realistic avenues by which we can achieve those plans that in no way depend on connections or politics. We still have challenges, but also have options for overcoming them. It may sound like I am mindlessly repeating vacuous statements about the American Dream, but compared to how hard achievement can be in Macedonia, it is easy to see why so many people leave in search of something more attainable if they can.

Living abroad also gave me a new perspective on some of the most pervasive stereotypes that people have about the United States. I learned that perhaps the most common misperception that outsiders have about Americans is that we know nothing about them and they know everything about us. While it is true that most Americans would struggle to find Macedonia, Serbia, or Albania on a map, it is equally true that most Macedonians would struggle to find Iowa, Vermont, or Kentucky on a map, and both groups of people would struggle to find Botswana, Indonesia, or Paraguay. There is some false sense of familiarity because American media is so dominant there, but very few people have any idea of what life is actually like in the United States, just as most Americans do not know what life is like in Macedonia. Likewise, Macedonians are likely to know more about US foreign policy than the average American, but Americans are likely to know more about domestic issues than the average Macedonian. In other words, both groups know the things that track closer to their immediate surroundings and personal interests.

Another common stereotype that I encountered is that Americans are unhealthier than the rest of the world because of rampant obesity, a penchant for fast food, and an aversion to exercise. In certain parts of the United States, that stereotype is a very present reality that lowers life expectancies and increases the cost of healthcare. In other parts of the country, however, obesity rates are on par with those in Europe, and in some places they are actually lower. While you won't see much morbid obesity in Macedonia, being out of shape and overweight is as common there as it is anywhere else. And while there are not any fast food drive-thrus in the country, there is plenty of drinking hard liquor and eating greasy meats and cheese at kafanas. Going to new fitness centers has become trendy in Skopje, and there is a fledgling running community, but even professional athletes smoke and drink in public. Health food is only now starting to catch on, and again it is hard to understate the pervasiveness of smoking, even among some people who go to the fitness center on a regular basis. My point is not to state that these things do not exist in the United States, but rather to point out that at the very least, we do not have the market cornered when it comes to unhealthy living.

Finally, living in Macedonia gave me insight into what it is like to experience globalization from a more nuanced perspective. The younger generation is more than eager to submit to the unstoppable steamroller that is globalization and finally experience all the things that they see on television and movies but never had. While that is certainly understandable, I also can't help but wonder what is being lost in the process. Macedonia opened its first modern mall as recently as 2012, and it has all of the empty charm of any mall located anywhere in the world. Despite that fact, the younger generation can't get enough of it, and would much rather sit for coffee there and pay more than double the price than be seen at some rundown local place with folk music blaring over the speakers.

As an outsider, it is not my place to tell people there what to do and where to go. Speaking for myself, I felt that the soul of the country is at a place where people sing as loud as they want at six in the evening, drink as much as they want for a price they can afford, and celebrate with a full heart. The seats may have cigarette burns and the tablecloths have holes and stains, but they also represent the heart and soul of a bygone time for which globalization has no place. It is in those types of places, and not in the malls and high-end coffee bars, where I felt transported to another place that was truly beautiful, truly unique, and truly Macedonian. In those moments, Macedonia really can feel like a paradise, when уживање (enjoying) takes precedence over the worries and cares of the world outside. For those types of experiences, I have yet to find any place better than Macedonia.

GLOSSARY

A Foreigner's Guide to Basic Macedonian

Ajde – an untranslatable word that can mean "come on," "let's go," "go ahead," or just "alright." Use it, it's fun. Could also mean something like "le le" (see below) if it is drawn out.
- Let's go get coffee. Ajde.
- Can I come in? Ajde.
- I'll see you later. Ajde.
- We're late. Ajde!
- My boss cut our salaries. Ajdeeeeeee...

Cirenje i kaskeval – literal translation would be cheese and cheese, but they refer to the two different types of cheese available in the Balkans: soft white or firm yellow. Americans might not appreciate the difference between these two things and consider them both to be just "cheese," but to them there is a big distinction. Both go great with rakija or wine.

Drustvo – literally means companionship, but could also refer to the process of hanging out with friends and good people.
- I had a great time last time, we had super *drustvo*.

Ima Plata! – the victory shout that you hear at work when people finally get paid after their salary was delayed for a few weeks or months and they are broke.

Kafana – something akin to a tavern that serves food. People go to a kafana for hours at a time and order multiple courses of food, starting with salads and cheeses and moving on to grilled meats (*skara*). This is a commitment; pace yourself. It's also probably the best thing Macedonia has going for it. There is often live music and dancing at the table.

Katastrofa – literally catastrophe, but useful to interject into essentially any conversation because the chances are, whatever the person is telling you will involve some sort of catastrophic situation.
- I didn't get paid for a month. Katastrofa.
- They are only hiring people with political party cards. Katastrofa.
- My in-laws are driving me nuts. Katastrofa.

Kromid i Luk – onions and garlic, staples of Macedonian cuisine, widely considered to be "the healthiest things you can eat," even if they are consumed with hard liquor and chased with a few cigarettes.

- Onions (or garlic) give the food taste! You can't eat X without onions (or garlic)!
- This has a little onion (or garlic) in it. It's really good for you!

Le le – also untranslatable, but can be thought of like "Oh my god!" in some instances, or like "Oh wow!" in others. You can add more le le's or draw out the second one to change the meaning, and add an Ajde or Katastrofa for good measure.
- Le le! Look how expensive this is! Le le!
- Le le le le le! What a beautiful baby!
- My landlord is evicting us. Le leeeeeee…. Katastrofa.

Makedonska rabota – a phrase to describe the prevailing way in which things function in Macedonia, also used to express a resigned sense of injustice
- I waited for three hours and the doctor never came. Makedonska rabota.
- Everyone is honking in traffic for no reason. Makedonska rabota.

Mekici – fried, unsweetened dough that can be eaten with soft white cheese, traditionally served when a new baby is born, but it is fine to eat mekici at other times as well.

Na Gosti – being a guest somewhere, or having people over, depending on the context. If people go *na gosti* at your place, you should have snacks, coffee, and drinks ready to go, and it wouldn't hurt to have an ash tray because they will smoke inside whether you do or not. Also, a guest might stay until well after midnight, even on a weeknight. They take this whole thing kind of seriously.

Na Kafe – meaning to get coffee with someone, this can be an hours long engagement that may or may not involve coffee. It is the institution at the center of all social life in the Balkans and not something to rush through. Because of the literal meaning of the phrase, you might hear Macedonian speakers say in English that they are "on coffee."
- Let's go "na kafe."
- Ajde na kafe.
- The Americans do not go to coffee (na kafe) like people in the Balkans, they are a cold, soulless people.

Narodna musika – meaning traditional music, or national music, this is the kind of music you are likely to hear at wedding celebrations when you are dancing in a circle.

Oro – the Balkan circle dance, for lack of a better description. It is pretty much the greatest wedding innovation since cake because the most basic form is easy, it gets everyone involved, and can be surprisingly fun. There are more advanced versions that require practice and prior knowledge, so when things start getting complicated, go have a rakija break.

Papuci – house slippers that people will offer you when you are *na gosti* whether you want them or not, they protect you from the relentless death grip of mysterious illnesses that come from having bare feet. Guests to your place will expect that you will *papuci* ready for them too.
-       Here are your papuci so you don't catch a cold, and any number of other strange illnesses that have nothing to do with the temperature of your feet.

Pauza – meaning break, as in from work, usually combined with coffee and cigarettes.
-       Where is everyone? On pauza.
-       No one seems to be working here, there is just a sign that says "pauza."

Peglica – slang term meaning "little iron" for the Fiat 126, which is quite possibly one of the smallest cars I have ever seen. Despite its diminutive size, a peglica often has a large luggage rack mounted on the top for people to strap down and transport any number of goods, including lightweight boats in the old days. Not recommended for anyone over 5'6".

Pivo – beer, your greatest friend. Southern Europe is not really a beer-drinking culture, wine and rakija are more their thing, so there is not much variety in terms of beer. The two big breweries in Macedonia produce Zlaten Dab and Skopsko, which are both quite similar in taste and are by far the most affordable options. A half-liter at most places in Skopje (as of early 2016) was about two dollars.

Promaja – draft or breeze, especially indoors, associated with any number of illnesses no matter how hot it is. No amount of logic or science will convince people that a breeze will not make you ill, so it's not worth trying.
- Close that window! There is a baby here we can't have a breeze (even though no one has air conditioning and it is over 90 degrees outside)!
- I got sick because these windows are drafty.

Rakija – a sort of Balkan brandy, this is the cure for what ails you. Also great for cleaning. Acceptable to drink at pretty much any time of the day, any day of the week, it goes great with salads and cheese. Also known as *"zolta,"* as in yellow, because of its color. There is a clear variety called *"bela,"* meaning white, but the word *rakija* implies the yellow variety.

- Let's have a rakija before we get back to work.
- Do you want a little rakija with that salad?

Skara – grilled meats, usually beef, pork, or chicken of different kinds, could also apply to kebabs, which are pretty much the greatest food in the Balkans. Side note: it is certainly possible to maintain a vegetarian diet in Macedonia, and according to the rules of the Orthodox Church people should even go vegan for almost one third of the year, but if you visit as a foreigner there will be a nearly endless offering of meats.

Slava – untranslatable, but means something like feast, as in a feast day in honor of a saint. Different families celebrate different slavas that were passed down through the family tree, and different customs are observed on each one. They generally involve lots of food and drink.

Sopska salata – a salad consisting of cucumbers, tomatoes, white soft cheese, and sometimes onions. Goes great with rakija, especially in the summer.

Uzhivanje – meaning enjoyment, or the feeling one gets when sitting at a kafana with friends around a table that is full of food and drink with live music playing in the background.

WC – pronounced V Tse, short for wash closet, as in bathroom. Kind of important.

About the Author

Benjamin Shultz is geographer by training and has taught at the University of Tennessee and International Balkan University in Skopje, Macedonia. He completed a Ph.D. in geography in 2011 and is now working to be a university administrator back in the United States. He is an avid runner, a dedicated fan of Kentucky basketball and Arsenal soccer, and a student of society.

Made in the USA
Middletown, DE
10 August 2016